Risky Strategy

Risky Strategy

Understanding Risk to Improve Strategic Decisions

Jamie MacAlister

Bloomsbury Business
An imprint of Bloomsbury Publishing Plc

B L O O M S B U R Y
LONDON · OXFORD · NEW YORK · NEW DELHI · SYDNEY

Bloomsbury Business
An imprint of Bloomsbury Publishing Plc

50 Bedford Square	1385 Broadway
London	New York
WC1B 3DP	NY 10018
UK	USA

www.bloomsbury.com

BLOOMSBURY and the Diana logo are trademarks of Bloomsbury Publishing Plc

First published 2016

British Library Cataloguing-in-Publication Data
A catalogue record for this book is available from the British Library.

ISBN: HB: 978-1-4729-2604-3
ePDF: 978-1-4729-2606-7
ePub: 978-1-4729-2605-0

Library of Congress Cataloging-in-Publication Data
Names: MacAlister, Jamie, author.
Title: Risky strategy : understanding risk to improve
strategic decisions / Jamie MacAlister.
Description: London ; New York : Bloomsbury Information Ltd, [2016] |
Includes bibliographical references and index.
Identifiers: LCCN 2016009026| ISBN 9781472926043 (hardback) |
ISBN 9781472926067 (epdf)
Subjects: LCSH: Strategic planning. | Risk. | Risk management. | Decision making.
Classification: LCC HD30.28 .M24 2016 | DDC 658.15/5–dc23
LC record available at https://lccn.loc.gov/2016009026

Cover image © A. Aleksandravicius / Getty Images

Typeset by Integra Software Services Pvt. Ltd.
Printed and bound in Great Britain

Contents

Chapter 1
Introduction: A tale of two cities

The two Steves, Wozniak and Jobs, created Apple Computer in 1976 and launched the first successful mass-produced microcomputer, the Apple II, at the West Coast Computer Faire in 1977. Wozniak designed it; Jobs oversaw the development. Wozniak was a highly analytical and methodical thinker; Jobs was an intuitive and impulsive decision maker. Wozniak was the elephant; Jobs was the tiger. Both engaged in the Apple risk story in different ways. Jobs the tiger may be the one we remember most, but he couldn't have done it without Wozniak the elephant.

Another risk story is the race to the South Pole in 1911. Scott took the well-explored longer route; Amundsen followed the unexplored shorter one. Scott used mainly ponies and snowmobiles; Amundsen used dogs. Scott had multiple objectives; Amundsen had only one – 'To be the first to the pole'. Amundsen came first and returned with all his team; Scott came second, and neither he nor his team survived. Both took risks – different risks for different reasons.

Charles Dickens (1859) tells us: It was the best of times in London; it was the worst of times in Paris. I've picked up on his theme of 'difference' and 'tension' in this book. He was referring to the time of the French Revolution, from which emerged two leaders who handled risk in very particular ways. Napoleon drove the English fleet out of Toulon by placing cannon strategically on a hill overlooking the harbour, which he himself helped take and ended up being wounded in the process; he understood artillery and English military history. Nelson defeated the French and Spanish fleets at Trafalgar by changing the rules of sea combat, heading straight for the middle of the enemy fleet and not engaging broadside on; he was an expert on the weather and the geometry of naval encounters but died in the experience. Both knew a lot about key variables. Both made bold choices to achieve winning results.

When it comes to working with risk, I believe a leader is a mediator. A leader needs to be able to work with tensions that pull in different directions, and, in spite of this, move followers forward resolutely. A leader needs to work with the 'cities'.

A leader needs to understand variability, and to make choices about that variability. A leader needs to know the variables that count. This is the essence of risk. Risk tends to be defined in different ways, which I will explore in more detail. However, for the main purpose of this book, and thinking about strategy making, risk is the level of variability of possible outcomes. Leaders need to understand and be able to work effectively with it.

The most important variable is character. A leader needs to understand character, both their own and that of their followers. Character defines not only how the leader works with risk, but also how the followers work with risk.

Strategy is about making choices that involve risk – being choiceful with risk and the implications of those choices. This is about selecting the right variables to work with, and the key to doing this is character.

In the final analysis, leaders need to feel safe with risk. It may be a paradox, but it has to happen. This book is about the journey towards feeling safe with risk, which is the key to effective strategy.

Working with the tensions

This is a book for aspiring leaders because it is about tensions, and the positive creativity that can emerge in addressing them: in pulling together differences, and in combining ideas and concepts that don't naturally sit together. It's a journey of discovery of what happens when you try to mix yin with yang; when you wonder if it's not yes or no, but po (this was the word that Edward de Bono proposed as an alternative to 'yes' or 'no' to encourage more creative thinking in addressing issues) (Bono, 1999) as a way of moving from the binary to the creative. The tension is what you feel when you stand in the gap, between the polarities. It's not always comfortable, but it's the place where I believe good things can flourish.

This was where I started when I decided to write a book that combined what I have learned in a career as a business strategy specialist, with what I have been discovering more recently about risk as a result of a research programme at Ashridge Business School. Straight away, these two concepts of 'strategy' and 'risk' create a tension – because the people who tend to work a lot with one of them tend to be different from the people who work with the other. And yet I have also discovered that business leaders seem to be interested in both.

Another tension emerges when you start to consider whether strategy is primarily about avoiding risk or taking it. And this is partly because there are underlying tensions in how we view and define risk. Risk is a curious subject in this regard. Sometimes it's an analytical concept leading to a pre-occupation with minimizing it; sometimes it's an intuitive idea and we are *thinking* about taking it. Sometimes it's about danger; at other times it's about opportunity. Sometimes we associate risk with variability; at other times with crisis. When we start to categorize it, we notice that financial risk is being usurped by reputational risk. And we confuse whether we are talking about risk to the organization, or the risk to us as individuals.

When we look at the psychology behind strategic decision making, we discover an intriguing tension between the desire to win and the need not to lose, and between the conflicting instincts to compete or to collaborate.

One of the long-standing debates is about how strategy squares with organizational capabilities. Some of the proposed approaches to strategy start with a looking-outwards perspective, while assessing capabilities involves looking inwards. Which one is driving which? Do capabilities help determine strategy, or does strategy drive capabilities? Most commentators would suggest the latter, on the basis that capabilities can be developed. That is until you throw organizational culture into the mix; that is not so easy to develop or change. 'Culture eats strategy for breakfast', apparently. There is clearly a tension here.

I have preferred to consider and develop the concept of 'organizational character' as a key factor in strategy. There is something about character which brings risk to the fore. Character is different from culture. Both are descriptions of the kind of human behaviours that are rewarded (or not) in an organization. But while culture is more a view of how things are, character is more a view of how things seek to be, or even need to be. And sometimes character is needed in order to avoid risk, and sometimes it requires the taking of risk. So I develop the idea of 'Risky Strategy' that is in tension with 'Organizational Character'.

I have chosen this 'tensions-based' opening to my book, because it brings back a formative memory of the first book that was read to me and my classmates by our school headmaster. Charles Dickens's *A Tale of Two Cities* (1859) starts with:

> *It was the best of times; it was the worst of times, it was the age of wisdom, it was the age of foolishness, it was the epoch of belief, it was the epoch of incredulity, it was the season of Light, it was the season of Darkness, it was the spring of hope, it was the winter of despair, we had everything before us, we had nothing before us, we were all going to Heaven, we were all going direct the other way.*

In a sense, this book is a tale of two cities: the cities of 'risk' and 'strategy'. Like Dickens's portrayal of London and Paris at the time of the French Revolution, our two cities have very different characters and yet the interplay between them creates an intriguing dynamic.

It is also the tale of two animals: the 'elephant' and the 'tiger', animals that tackle risk in very different ways.

I have chosen to recount the stories of recent history and more distant history, looking at risk and strategy from not only a business perspective, but from a sports one, a military one and a scientific one. The interplay between France and England, which is the backdrop of Dickens's novel, is also the backdrop of the exploits of Napoleon and Nelson, who were in turn well-documented examples of the growing art of military strategy – lessons on which I will draw in this book.

I also hear this juxtaposition of contrasting ideas ringing in my memory of the lines of King Solomon, set out in the Book of Ecclesiastes:

> *A time to embrace,*
> *And a time to refrain from embracing*
> *A time to gain,*
> *And a time to lose*

And I am reminded of tensions between collaboration and competition, and of the psychology of winning versus that of avoiding losing. These are all key themes in this book. They impact business purpose or mission, which, in turn, is what drives business strategy. They mould our view on what is the right risk to take when making strategic decisions.

My hypothesis is that great leadership is at least in part about being able to work with these tensions, that somehow the collision of these tensions involves risk and, at the same time, brings new creation. I will introduce you to a model I created called the Blonay Character Profiler, which is based on tensions in character attributes, and suggest that understanding these is at the heart of the great chemistry in leadership which can in turn harness individual potential.

Later in this book, I'll introduce you to a concept I call 'Creative Juxtaposition', which I believe is at the heart of innovative strategic decisions. It's the cousin of a concept I borrowed from William Duggan, a professor at Columbia Business School, which he calls 'Strategic Intuition'. He, in turn, borrowed some of his thinking from von Clausewitz's work on military strategy, who had observed Napoleon from a distance.

I also need to tell you that this book is a journey, for me and I hope for you, the reader. It's a journey that begins here, but I'm afraid doesn't end within the confines of this book. If you are looking for a book that gives you the answers to all your questions about risk and strategy, then I would suggest you stop here, for you will be disappointed. My hope is that this book asks a number of good questions that may help you think differently about how you approach strategic decision making.

Later in the book, I draw on a concept called 'Intelligent Ignorance', and that is the basis of our journey. What would be a great result from this book would be the beginning of a community, perhaps linking up on a social media platform, all of whom share a similar intelligent ignorance about the questions raised by this book.

I welcome you on this journey which starts here, and look forward to the possibility of walking with you, as the journey extends beyond ...

What this book offers you as a leader

If you want to make progress, because you can't be in control of everything, you need to be aware of risk ... Risk is the core skill of leadership. (CEO of a London Hospital Trust)

My contention is that being able to work with the risk associated with tough 'strategic' decisions, and to work effectively with the tensions I have just described, associated with that process, is a core skill of leadership.

One of the questions we asked respondents in our research on risk was, 'How do you think an organization that dealt perfectly with risk would look?' To which the CEO of a media company, with whom I spoke, responded, 'Well, it wouldn't need me, for starters! That is what I believe I am paid to take care of.'

So this book is essentially about effective decision making under uncertainty – which is what the future offers us. The conundrum is that because these kinds of decisions by definition have long-term consequences, we often don't know how effective they are until it is too late to change them. So I can't offer any long-term guarantees about the outcomes of those decisions. So what can we offer for now?

As previously stated, in this book, I am asking you to join me on a journey to explore what we can learn in this area. My sources, which I describe in more detail in the next section, are a combination of our own research into how leaders work with risk, what others have written on risk and strategy, and my own experience in both leadership roles and roles advising clients on strategy. On this journey, I seek to answer the following questions:

1. When and in what sense is strategy making risky, and how do I evaluate when to take risk and when to seek to avoid it? (Chapter 2)
2. What aspects of the character of my organization, the extent to which it embraces risk, could influence strategy? (Chapter 3)
3. How do we think about and define risk? (Chapter 4)
4. What are the different approaches to dealing with risk? (Chapters 5 and 6)
5. What mind games might be influencing the way I evaluate risk? (Chapter 7)
6. How does my approach to winning and being competitive influence my approach to risk? (Chapter 8)
7. How does the way I work with information and understand variability impact my decision making? (Chapter 9)

8. What is the connection between risk and innovation? (Chapter 10)
9. How should I work with reputational risk, and deal with the possibility of crisis? (Chapter 11)
10. What aspects of the character of the organization work best with risk? (Chapter 11)
11. How can I feel safe with risk? (Chapter 12)

Much clever stuff has been written about the management of risk. Part of the purpose of this book is to make the consideration of risk more accessible and understandable to those senior managers involved in setting strategy, those of you with busy lives that don't necessarily have a PhD in advanced psychology or mathematics. Part of it is to help develop a common language and understanding for talking about it. More 'risky' conversation is part of the answer to working well with risk, and I believe that this will help leaders to reach better and more effective decisions.

I have set out to eliminate technical language or acronyms, sometimes referred to as jargon, which may hinder your understanding of what I am trying to say. Where I can't think of another short way to express a particular technical concept, I will use it but generally assume that you are not necessarily fully aware of what the concept means, and seek to explain what it means. Of course, the flip side is that, for some of you, what I write may seem rather facile and this issue may put you off. It's one of the risks I have chosen to take in writing this book. I'm practising what I'm preaching in choosing my risks!

My story and my sources

This book draws from a combination of research into how leaders and organizations work with risk and strategy, and my own experience.

At Ashridge Executive Education, now part of the Hult International Business School, I have been involved in research into how risk is really managed. We looked extensively at the literature, often involving complex financial modelling or psychological theories, and we talked to managers in senior leadership roles about how they work with risk. We reported on this in 2014, and I cover the highlights from this report in

Chapter 4. I have also recently been looking at the risks associated with modern slavery in the global supply chain for major retailers (following the passing of the recent UK Modern Slavery Act into law) – and I talk more about that in Chapter 3.

Prior to coming to Ashridge, I had been a strategy consultant for twenty-one years, in the early years with PwC and latterly with my own consultancy business. In my experience of teaching business strategy concepts, and working with senior management teams on developing strategy, risk is often mentioned in passing, but rarely forms a core part of the strategy decision-making process. This is perhaps surprising, as strategy is about making decisions that concern the future, and an uncertain future at that, and therefore where risk should play a significant role.

Having also held leadership roles myself, I have my own thoughts on why this might be. One factor is clearly the difference on how we view risk – how we define it even. In our research, we picked this up and characterized it as either a formal analytical 'elephant' approach, which tends to be more risk averse, or an informal intuitive 'tiger' approach, which tends to be risk taking.

Apart from setting up my own consultancy business, I have been involved in setting up two social enterprises in the UK, and in developing a charitable educational venture in Uganda. In each case, I see these different approaches to risk manifest themselves in different ways, as regards my approach compared to that of others. I have a role on the board of both social enterprises, but in one my role is very much as the intuitive 'tiger' seeking to encourage further adventure while my colleagues take a more considered approach. As one of the two initial investors and founders, I am manifesting more of the behaviour that got that the enterprise started in the first place. In the other social enterprise, I have the opposite role, that of caution to my 'tiger' colleague, Pete, who is the primary inspiration and energy behind the venture. But in this role, my value has been realized in taking different kinds of risks – tough decisions to close aspects of the enterprise to avoid bankruptcy.

I am intrigued by these dynamics that I have witnessed first-hand, and this is one aspect that has driven the writing of this book. I am also intrigued by the various ideas in the literature on both strategy and risk, some of which have been pillars of wisdom in my time as a strategy consultant, and some of which is relatively new to me.

As regards strategy, this book will cherry-pick what I consider the best of the essence of writing on strategy, drawing from the great military strategic writers like von Clausewitz, to the more recent classical business strategy texts from the likes of Michael Porter (1980), Igor Ansoff (1965), Treacy and Wiersema (1995), Kim and Mauborgne (2005), Jim Collins (2001), David Teece (2011) and Henry Mintzberg (1994). I am particularly impressed by the more pragmatic views on strategy making expressed by A. G. Lafley, the former CEO of Procter & Gamble, in partnership with Roger Martin (2013), and by my Ashridge colleague Stephen Bungay (2011), who draws business lessons from the great military strategist von Clausewitz.

The book will also draw from both the analytical and the intuitive side of risk-based decision making. In understanding the subtleties of each mode, we will draw from the work of Daniel Kahneman (2011) and Malcolm Gladwell (2006). We will explore what these and others like Nassim Taleb (2010) and Andrew Campbell et al. (2008) have to say on how, if we are not careful, we can get risk-related decisions all wrong.

These all approach strategy and risk from slightly different perspectives, and I think a really interesting thing starts to happen when you pull them together and compare them. In one sense, it's an uncomfortable place, somehow straddling the views of great minds, and seeking either to reconcile or disagree. In another sense, it is hugely revealing – the synergistic effect creates something new. And in this point, the most interesting of all the texts that I draw from is the work of William Duggan on *Strategic Intuition* (2007), in which he draws lessons not only from business and military strategists, but also from science, art and religion, to describe a synthesizing approach to creating and implementing strategy.

I build on Duggan's work through a concept that came to mind some years ago, which I now feel able to embellish – that of 'Creative Juxtaposition'. I think this process is at the heart of innovation and new knowledge, and is, I believe, part of what is happening with Strategic Intuition.

In turn, another part of this process is 'Intelligent Ignorance', covered in the work of Stuart Firestein (2012). And underlying all this is character – both individual character but also how that relates to organizational character, which is at the heart of strategy. Character attributes around boldness and courage, which lead to risk taking, vie for dominance with other character attributes such as humility and empathy, or integrity and disciplined structured thinking. I will introduce you to the Blonay Character Profiler (MacAlister 2015), a tool I developed a number of years ago to support my strategy practice, which helps individuals consider their own character biases.

Chapter 2

When strategy gets risky

Strategy is risky. That's why most business managers don't do proper strategy.

The extent to which you agree with both of these statements probably depends in part on how you define the word 'strategy' and how you define 'risky' or 'risk'. We know that, like many commonly used words, they often can mean different things to different people, or their generally accepted meanings can change over time. Such, I believe, is true of these two words.

So, firstly, I will outline what I mean by these words, and then we can explore briefly how their meanings might differ or may have changed over time.

'Strategy' is about being deliberate in committing resource to do certain things in the future, in order to achieve particular outcomes or consequences. It involves making choices about what you are going to do, and therefore, either explicitly or by implication, what you are not going to do. This last part is important because these choices involve resources that are generally limited in terms of their availability, whether that is your time, actions, energy and money or other peoples' time, actions, energy and money. So by being deliberate about what you are going to do, you therefore exclude what you are not going to do. I define it like this because, in my experience, only a strategy that has this attribute can have any real value.

I don't think strategy necessarily refers to actions that are conducted over a long period of time. You can have a strategy for a particular meeting or how to handle a specific current issue. The point is about being deliberate and committed, having limited resource and aiming for a specific outcome.

So what about risk? In this book, I explore different views and definitions of risk, but my main proposition is to define it in the same way as financial analysts view risk: as the perceived variability of possible harm or benefit of outcome, resulting from a certain decision or action. The outcome can be either positive or negative, and risk is the extent to which it could be either. A 'risky' decision means there is more variability of benefit of outcome resulting from that decision than from an alternative 'non-risky' decision. By implication, it means that there is more variability from undertaking a certain action than there is from not undertaking that action. This definition of risk I shall refer to as the 'variability definition'.

This, however, is not the most common understanding of risk, which is generally associated more single-mindedly with danger, and defined more like the impact and likelihood of harm resulting from an action. In terms of overall understanding, risk is generally associated with a negative benefit of outcome: the likelihood and impact of something bad happening. This alternative understanding I shall refer to as the 'danger definition'.

However, it is more helpful for the understanding of the nature of risk to consider it as a measure of variability, positive or negative, from an expected outcome. It should become clear as you read on as to why this is a more helpful definition.

Crossing a road

So, to kick off, let's look next at the example of 'crossing a road' to develop what I am saying. In this example, I would define risk as the variability of benefit arising from two possible outcomes: either being hit by a car or reaching the other side of the road – this is the extent of variability of possible outcomes. The more generally accepted understanding of risk would just be the likelihood of the negative benefit (or cost) of being hit by a car, according to the danger definition. This action is 'risky' based on the variability definition because, in taking this action, the variability of benefit ranges between some likelihood of each of these two outcomes, whereas by not crossing the road, the likelihood of either of those outcomes is substantially reduced.

So, if I define strategy as being deliberate about doing things in the future, then why is it risky, according to the variability definition? The answer is that we have less knowledge about the future than we do about the present, so making choices about actions in the future makes those actions inherently more risky (i.e. there is a higher variability of possible outcomes) than making choices about those in the present.

To understand this point, let's go back to our road-crossing analogy. I can make a decision, in the present, to cross the road. The information I need to minimize the risk is whether or not there are any cars approaching this place at this time. If not, then I cross the road and the range of possible outcome benefits is limited pretty much to a positive outcome: my successfully getting to the other side of the road unharmed.

However, if I make the choice now to cross the road in exactly five minutes time, I am making a deliberate choice about an action in the future. I can probably estimate, based on what I have been observing while I have been at the side of the road, how likely it is that there is a car approaching at that time. But if I stick to my decision to cross the road in exactly five minutes time, regardless of what I may observe about oncoming cars at the time, then there is a much higher likelihood of being hit by a car, so the variability of possible outcomes is higher, so the risk is higher. Therefore, having a strategy, according to my definition, is in this instance more risky than not having a strategy. Strategy is risky.

So this illustration would clearly raise the question: why have a strategy according to this definition? This is linked to another question: why take risk?

In the next chapters, I shall explore these ideas. And I will be looking at how you evaluate and understand risk in the context of strategy. This touches on the issue of where are risks real and imagined? What are the benefits to a group or organization in understanding and working with risk more effectively, together? And at the end of the day, as leaders, how do we assess what are the right risks to take?

Why strategies don't make choices

In my time as a strategy consultant, I probably worked with in excess of 100 organizations, engaged in some aspect of strategy. I can't think of a single case where I thought, 'Wow, this organization has a really useful and effective strategy!'

Of course, in some cases, that was the reason why I was there, and in those cases, I cannot put my hand on my heart and say that what we came up with was the 'best thing since sliced bread'. By the way, I am guessing that idiom probably needs explaining or changing, as I am not sure that sliced bread is that good, nor was it ever. There were various reasons for that which I will explain in a bit.

Often I inherited some kind of strategy which was already in place, and needed either to be developed further, or there was some issue with its implementation. On other occasions, there was either no strategy at all, or I would get a different answer depending on whom I asked as to what the organization's strategy was.

In one intriguing case, my client had invested in a major system implementation, and wanted our team to develop a strategy which would support the case for the investment and how it would deliver benefit. While the client was clear that this might not ideally have been the right way round, I thought at least they were, in a way, honest about it. I think a lot of strategies are developed to support major decisions that have already been taken. This has echoes of a phenomenon called 'cognitive inertia' which I cover in more depth in Chapter 7, where I cover illusions and traps that can impede our ability to assess risk effectively. Some would argue that this is a valid way to approach strategy making – primarily driven by what we already have in terms of capability, which in turn is driven by decisions we have already taken.

My 100 plus clients have been organizations of all shapes and sizes: private, public or third sector; from major multinationals to small family businesses; different industry sectors; and different countries. Overall, what I have found is that strategies do not generally drive or even influence many of the decisions in the business, at least not overtly. What I mean is that leaders will make major decisions that are largely pragmatic, occasionally supported by some kind of financial case, often supported by some kind of intuition of a leader or common view of a leadership team. And while the strategy may provide some background comfort to the decision maker, it has little impact on the decision.

And I have given some degree of thought as to why that might be. And largely, I believe it is to do with the quality of the strategy, in whatever way it is articulated.

The biggest issue with strategies in the organizations that I have come across is that they don't actually make any serious decisions. 'We aim to be the leading player in this industry by delivering high quality products at a competitive price with reliable customer service, using the best people and processes we can achieve ...' isn't a helpful strategy statement. I can't imagine any leader in the business saying to themselves, 'We were going to deliver a low quality product, but we changed our mind because of the strategy.'

So this begs the following question: Why don't strategy makers often make serious decisions? I believe the answer is probably something along the lines of: 'We are dealing with the future. The future is uncertain. So it's hard to be confident that what we decide now will still be valid when we come to implement a key decision. So we had better not decide now.'

The fault is in the process many organizations go through to make strategy. And this is often driven by what business schools have been telling them is the right way to develop strategy. Some leaders have been taught that it is a linear, largely analytical process which doesn't really deal head-on with the issue of uncertainty. It is generally not skilled, and therefore probably not comfortable with dealing with the subject of risk.

Let us describe a caricature of a typical strategy making process.

Linear strategic thinking

I would say that strategy making typically consists of a linear process with a series of key steps. I know this because as a strategy consultant, fairly well read and taught in the art of strategy making, I have, on a number of occasions, proposed a process somewhat along these lines. Today, I question how helpful this approach is.

A typical process would look something like:

1. Define mission, vision, aspiration or problem statement
2. Analyse: performance, market, customers, competitors

3. Examine internal strengths and weaknesses/sources of competitive advantage
4. Formulate options – and possibly criteria for assessing options (use of various tools to support this – pyramid approach, priority setting)
5. Produce financial models with scenarios
6. Work with stakeholders to agree preferred option
7. Consider risks in preferred option and ways of mitigating those risks
8. Develop a supporting plan with financials, milestones, etc.
9. Produce a summary document

It actually all seems quite logical, which is probably why my being quite a logical person, I have been happy to propose such a process.

The main issue with this is that while a lot of organizations may follow a process like this, when we look at organizations that have prospered, this type of process has had very little to do with the reasons for their success.

More specifically, a problem with this process is that risk, step 7 in the process, is treated as a bit of an afterthought.

The problem is in the implementation, or is it?

I have just spent a day with a global client in a programme session with over a 100 of their most senior managers. It kicked off with a presentation on the new strategy for the business. I heard a well-argued technical case for the aspiration for the business – what the business needed to do more of and less of. There was a general sense of nodding in agreement, and the rest of the day was spent in group discussions about what needed to change in the business. I had a sense that it was an excellent day with many useful conversations about changes. But at the end of the day, I was left with a question in my mind, which I imagine might have been in the minds of others in the room. To what extent did the changes that were talked about during the day have anything to do with the strategy that was presented at the beginning of the day?

I'd had a similar experience only the week before, when another strategy was presented. In this meeting, one of the employees asked the brave question that I think was on many minds: 'So that's great, but what do you want me to do?'

My colleague Stephen Bungay tells a similar story on implementing strategy in his book *The Art of Action* (2011), the story of a senior manager on hearing a similarly excellent presentation on strategy by the CEO, being brave enough to ask the 'so what do you want me to do?' Bungay argues that grappling with this problem is the real issue in strategy making. He draws extensively from von Clausewitz's work on military strategy, and even more extensively through the achievements of von Moltke, an effective German general in the nineteenth century.

I explore more of his argument in Chapter 9, 'Synthesis and key variables'. The point here is that what he calls friction, and what I will later develop more as 'variables' are what gets in the way of effective implementation of strategy.

He argues that the role of the overall leader therefore is to clarify what the overall mission is, the strategic intent, and to get engagement on that. And then the rest of the decisions are taken lower in the organization, where the gaps are effectively a lot smaller: the information is clearer, the people that need to implement are close and the local command can see the results of actions more quickly and respond more quickly.

This suggests that the answer to our senior manager's original question – 'What do you want me to do?' – is 'That's for you to figure out'. That may be right in its complete sense. But if the question was rephrased slightly as 'So what are the implications of this strategy for what I do?' is still answered in the same way, then I would suggest that the problem is not in the implementation; it is in the strategy itself.

Another colleague at one of the meetings I mentioned above expressed his reaction slightly differently: 'So this is all the stuff we are going to do. I'm already doing loads. What's going to give? What do we not do?'

Even the largest companies must make explicit choices to compete in some places, with some products, for some customers (and not in others). A choice to serve everyone, everywhere – or to simply serve all customers –

is a losing choice. Choosing about where to play is also about choosing where not to play. This is more straightforward when you are considering where to expand (or not), but considerably harder when you are considering if you should stay in the places and segments you currently serve.

Consider a company like General Electric. A decade ago it derived considerable revenue from its entertainment holdings and materials businesses. Today it has remade its portfolio to focus much more on infrastructure, energy and transportation, where its distinctive capabilities can make a real difference to winning. This was an explicit choice of where *not* to play (Lafley & Martin, 2013).

Steve Jobs articulated a similar idea: 'I'm as proud of what we don't do as what we do' (Steve Jobs on Apple's focus) (Johnson et al., 2014).

In my view, strategic decisions need to address some of the variables head-on. My sense is that where strategy is effective, that's what it does. It takes on some of the friction problems, rather than keep the drive speed and direction flexible, so that friction has less to resist. It addresses risk.

Risk management as an afterthought

I can remember on many occasions pulling together a strategy document, or a business plan, or a proposal for some kind of strategic decision, only to be challenged by an enlightened colleague saying to me: 'So what are the risks in what you are proposing? And how would we deal with those risks?' Risk typically was not even on my radar as I was crafting my brilliant thesis for what we should do.

So now I have learned that this question will come up, and I include a section on risk. It may be towards the rear of the document, or it may be an appendix, but at least I have thought about it. Even though it might be a bit of an afterthought.

And how do I approach this appendix section on risk? It will probably be a process something along the lines of:

1. Brainstorm/list possible risks by category (e.g. reputational, financial, market, operational, supply, legal, environmental, hazard).

2. Get information about risks (e.g. likelihood, severity).
3. Produce either a risk mitigation plan or a risk contingency plan for each risk.

Judging by other similar documents I have read by other authors, I don't think I am alone in this type of approach. Risk management is often a bit of an afterthought, at least that's the way it seems to read. We have come up with a great plan, for which there are a load of good reasons for doing it. But just in case anyone is interested in what might go wrong, we have covered that base, listed what the risks might be, and discussed what we would do about them.

It all sounds quite sensible. So what's the problem? Well, when it comes to strategy making at least, it doesn't seem to lead to good strategy making, for the reasons I have outlined. We end up with a strategy document that is not worth the paper on which it's written.

More to the point, this doesn't appear to be the way successful organizations actually work. Neither does it appear to be how successful ventures get delivered.

So, next, let's look a bit more at some examples of successful organizations, and some less successful ones, and consider whether there is an indication of the different ways they approach strategy and risk.

A closer look at success and failure

When we think of successful organizations in the business world, we typically think of businesses like Apple, Microsoft, Google, Intel, Virgin, Dyson and Toyota. These are relatively recent examples of success in terms of consistent profitable growth.

As we look longer term, we may think of organizations that have been around a long time and continue to prosper. I think of the business where I cut my marketing and strategy teeth, Procter and Gamble (P&G), which was founded in the middle of the nineteenth century on principles and a vision that still remain largely unchanged today.

When I think of failures, I typically think of organizations, or organizational brands at least, that are no longer with us: Kodak, Fisons, ICI, Barings Bank or Lehman Brothers.

I think it's also worth looking at organizations that have had to change significantly, and have now emerged out of the change as strong organizations. IBM is one such organization that comes to mind.

I can take a cursory look at these examples, some of which I have more in-depth knowledge of than others, and make some observations on how the successful ones approach strategy and risk, compared to the less successful ones.

But others have done a significantly more thorough job than I in comparing the good with the not-so-good, although not specifically on this topic.

I am thinking of the research that Jim Collins and colleagues have done to understand what is behind successful businesses compared to less successful ones. He did this most famously in his book *Good to Great* (2001). He records the results of research of 1,435 companies, where the 11 best performing companies outperformed the rest by 6.9 times the stock market average over fifteen years. He then analyses what factors distinguish the eleven successful companies compared to the rest. One of the findings is the character attributes of leaders in those successful companies, one of which is what he calls fortitude which is in essence the ability and resolve to take and stick to brave decisions – that is, risky decisions.

It's probably not sensible to have a serious look at what successful and unsuccessful strategies look like without examining some military history. Probably the best documented example of successful strategy making is that of Napoleon Bonaparte, thanks in part to the military strategy writer von Clausewitz. Napoleon cut his teeth and rode to fame as a leader at the Siege of Toulon, at which he proposed a strategy that was initially ignored by his superiors but eventually proved successful in getting the British fleet to leave Toulon. William Duggan in his book *Strategic Intuition* (2007) summarizes this event as a great example of Coup D'Oeil, von Clausewitz's term for the way good strategy is often made. I will develop this in greater depth later.

In looking further at military strategic decision-making successes and failures, it is interesting to compare two military campaigns in the Second World War, the Normandy D-Day invasion and Operation Market Garden, the Allies' attempt to capture three river bridges in the Netherlands. The Normandy landing in June 1944 had led to the destruction of two German armies in France and, although costly, was considered a success. However, Operation Market Garden was considered a failure in that the Allies were unable to capture the third bridge, Arnhem. The historian Max Hastings summed it up 'Market Garden was a rotten plan, poorly executed'. My Ashridge colleague Andrew Campbell and friends do a great job at analysing the reasons for this failure in their book *Think Again* (Campbell et al., 2008).

Another success story is the transformation of IBM from a primarily product manufacturing business to a services business. Much of the story is told between 1993 and 2002 by the CEO of IBM Louis Gerstner in his book *Who Says Elephants Can't Dance?* (n.d.). I develop this story in more depth in Chapter 10, which covers the subject of strategic pioneering. For now, it's worth noting that the nadir of his story is the two 'big bets' made by the business in the1990s, on the importance of IT-related business services, and on the move to networked IT solutions for businesses. Gerstner was brought in as CEO by the board to 'Save IBM'. Nearly ten years later, he resigned having successfully established IBM as a major global business services organization. This was consolidated by IBM's acquisition of one of the largest management consultancy businesses, PwC Consulting.

And I cannot complete my account of business success stories without mentioning an organization where I spent three and a half years learning more about how to be an effective business manager than at any other point in my life. That organization is Procter & Gamble (P&G), not so much a heroic story due to dramatic growth from a standing start, nor as a stunning transformation, but more because of sustained growth over a long business history stretching back to the middle of the nineteenth century. I have already described P&G's approach to advertising strategy, and we will explore more of P&G's approach to strategy when we think about winning aspirations later in the book.

SMaC's deliver results

Jim Collins and Morten Hansen, in their book *Great by Choice* (2011), talk about SMaC recipes, which they describe as Specific, Methodical and Consistent recipes. In this book, they extend the insightful analysis from Collins's book *Good to Great* to environments with high levels of uncertainty, and effectively ask how successful organizations make decisions compared to 'twinned', less successful organizations.

They conclude that the successful organizations develop SMaC recipes in order to make tough decisions about how they plan to operate, and generally stick to them in the face of a changing marketplace.

Howard Putnam, the CEO of Southwest Airlines, outlined a SMaC recipe in 1979 in the face of deregulation. This included aspects such as a focus on short-haul, using the Boeing 737 as the primary aircraft, fast turnarounds, low fares, no food service and a focus on keeping employees happy. The irony was that many of these ideas were copied from Pacific Southwest Airlines (PSA), but while Southwest Airlines stuck to their formula, PSA changed theirs. The result: Southwest Airlines has outperformed PSA financially by several multiples.

Intel developed a recipe based on Moore's law of increasing complexity (named after co-founder Gordon Moore): consistent R&D, standardized manufacturing, pricing cycles, service and constructive debating. It has stuck to this recipe through massive change in the semiconductor manufacturing market, and it continues to prosper.

Apple restored its earlier growth track when Steve Jobs returned to the helm, claiming that 'Apple's DNA hasn't changed'. This included such recipe items as design-friendly and elegant products, a focus on individuals not businesses, control of the primary technology, an obsession about secrecy and big launches to generate excitement.

One of their concluding comments in the book is that 'greatness is first and foremost a matter of conscious choice and discipline'. Another is: 'We've found in all our research studies that the signature of mediocrity is not an unwillingness to change; the signature of mediocrity is chronic inconsistency'. The only thing they claim is that SMaC recipes are not a strategy. I'm not sure why they felt this to be the case.

Strategy is reducing risk or is it?
The core process story

A little while ago, I had a discussion with a colleague of mine on the faculty at Ashridge, in which he proposed that the point of strategy making is to reduce risk to the organization. I understand his argument. Part of the strategy process is to look at what we are good at and what we are not so good at. Doing what we are good at is relatively low risk; trying to do what we are not so good at is high risk. This thinking can apply to the markets we operate in, the technologies we work with, the products or services we seek to offer customers and the processes that we engage with.

This is a particularly interesting argument when we apply it to processes. Some years ago, thanks to the work of Hamel and Prahalad (1990), and Hammer and Champy (1991), there was a lot of interest in businesses defining their core processes or competencies, and taking the view that processes that were not core were candidates for outsourcing. Normally, the business case was based on reducing costs. My colleague would have argued that it was also about reducing risk – leave what you are not so good at to others who are better at it.

I was working with PwC at the time, as a management consultant, and process re-engineering was a core part of our practice. As the strategy consultant on the team, part of my remit was to help define what the core processes were from a strategic perspective. There were some fascinating case studies of organizations that had done this, and sometimes come up with some not-so-obvious results. For example, when McDonald's looked at the issue, there was all sorts of speculation as whether it was about efficient catering, or even sourcing materials, or recruitment and training. The conclusion was that their core process was 'acquiring retail sites'. And of course, when you stop to think of it, it makes a lot of sense. They do seem to be good at finding the most impactful and convenient locations, which, as we all know, is the key to retailing.

We did the exercise at PwC, and concluded that the core process was recruiting and developing people. It would probably be the same for most professional services organizations. It wasn't managing projects with clients; it wasn't developing great ways of solving client problems. It wasn't financial management, perhaps surprising for a firm whose roots are in accountancy. In the light of this, it was perhaps not so surprising that PwC outsourced parts of its own financial management processes. It was supposedly lower cost, and probably lower risk, to get others to do this for us.

So there is clearly some sense to this idea of strategy being able to reduce risk. Another aspect to risk reduction through outsourcing is replacing a largely fixed cost (salaried employees) with a variable cost. A lot of outsourcing contracts are paid for, at least in part, on a fee-per-activity basis. This reduces risk by reducing the variability of profit margin, as activity levels fluctuate. I develop this idea further when I look in more depth at financial gearing in Chapter 5. If this logic doesn't quite work for you, you'll pick up more of an explanation later. For now, you will need to trust me that this does indeed reduce financial risk.

However, if we extend the analysis of the outsourcing process further, we know that there are many cases of organizations outsourcing processes to service organizations in the developing world, particularly in Asia. The business case for these strategic decisions has nearly always been about cost reduction, picking up significantly lower labour costs in these countries. However, in many of these cases, the risks to the business have arguably increased. There was undoubtedly more uncertainty at the outset as to how well these service organizations would perform. Businesses experienced more variability in service levels. Realizing the downside of these risks has led to some reversing their decisions, and bringing the processes either home, or in-house, or both. Others persevere as, for now, the risks do not outweigh the cost advantages.

The following question is pertinent: Was it appropriate to make a strategic decision that meant lower cost but higher risk? In my view, the answer is unequivocally yes. There is a risk-return evaluation that needs to be made, and this is at the heart of the strategic decision-making process. The same applies to the decision as to whether to enter new markets, or develop new technologies for new products and services, which almost by definition may not be in areas which you would count as core strengths.

Strategy making may or may not be about reducing risk to the organization. What is clear is that risk needs to be central to the strategy-making process.

Strategy for managers, risk for experts

Strategy making in organizations is ubiquitous. By that I mean that anyone in any kind of leadership role typically wants a piece of the process, and feels it's part of their responsibility. Most are not particularly good at it – some will admit it, some typically don't. It's not surprising that managers are generally not that good at it; by definition, it's not something managers do every day. It's why strategy consultancies can do well, charging clients to help them develop it. It's why strategy teaching is near the top of the pile of important topics at business schools. It's why books like this can hopefully sell quite well!

As I reported earlier in the book, views on what a strategy is will vary enormously – even in business schools. This is part of what makes it interesting. When I started out as a management consultant, I was part of what was then the Deloitte Haskins and Sells Marketing Consultancy. Amongst other things, we helped clients with marketing strategy. My colleagues had a healthy scepticism about how different clients viewed strategy and the value that we could add in helping them develop strategy. The word 'strategy' tended to get so abused, in their view, that at one point we all agreed that when any of us felt we were about to say the word 'strategy', we would say the word 'cake' instead. This was just to check that we really meant it when we said it, or whether in fact, there was a better way of saying what we were trying to say. I don't think we went as far as using this approach in front of clients – it was more of a back office thing. As far as I can remember, it worked well in getting us to be a bit more disciplined in how we used the word. The good news and the bad news about this is that it has stayed with me ever since, and I still think of cake when people talk about strategy. The good news is that it keeps me disciplined. The bad news is that it adversely affects my diet.

The point is that strategy is generally something that managers are happy discussing, agreeing and feeling responsible for. Much less so with risk, it would appear. Risk is for experts. It's why large company boards have separate committees, specifically tasked with looking at risk. It's why these same companies probably have a department or a management role looking specifically at risk. Or at the very least, it is part of the responsibilities that belong to the finance director. Or there is a special process looking at assessing different types of risk, and recommending what we do about it. This is generally quite separate from any strategic decision-making process. If a manager produces a proposal or plan of some kind, there will generally be some 'specialist'-type manager who asks 'Have we considered the risks?' often enough so that we get better at making sure that the plan includes an appendix that looks at risks. But we don't feel comfortable writing it, because it really feels like a specialist thing.

It's why we insure more and more things. It used to be just about disasters at sea, and then all kinds of possible accidents. Now we insure against the possibility that poor weather may stop play, or the chance that poor management judgement or even bad behaviour causes some kind of damage. Why? Partly because insurance companies are experts.

But strategic decisions are about uncertainty, which can otherwise be defined as risk. So it does seem a little strange that we, as strategy makers, don't pay more attention to it. One of the reasons possibly has something to do with the word 'risk' as opposed to the word 'uncertainty', which we shall cover in more depth in Chapter 4. There is something dodgy about risk.

Risk is taboo

As a passenger, have you ever been on a plane and asked a member of the cabin crew, at the start of a flight, about the risk of some kind of accident during the flight.

I have once, and got a very cool: 'I'd prefer not to talk about that if you don't mind'. I've never asked the question again. I imagine I would get a similar response, and that this would be a common response. And on reflection, I think I can understand why. If you are doing that particular job full time, all the time, you'd really rather not be talking about the likelihood of it all going badly wrong, all the time. And I think there's an element of superstition attached to it. There's some sixth sense that says: 'We don't talk about this kind of stuff... because in doing so, we are just inviting trouble!'

Back to the cabin crew issue: I understand their aversion to talking about it. But on the other hand, I think this question of mine just followed the routine explanation and demonstration of what to do in the case of some kind of accident. So in a way, it seems natural to ask the question. It's a question that most people, for whom it's one of the first times they have flown in an aeroplane, are quietly thinking they would like to have answered. Or are they? I don't know. Over to you.

I suspect there is something of this in why we don't look at risk more openly when we are making decisions, particularly strategic ones which involve us committing time and effort from a number of different people to some approach or course of action.

Part of the problem is that risk generally speaks to us of danger, that is, the possibility of harm. It's part of the heritage of the word. And exploring this in any depth at the point we are considering some decision which may imply some significant change seems to somehow to be starting off on the wrong foot! There is a sense that we are looking for trouble – almost in a superstitious sense.

Or at the very least, we are prompting a mindset in our audience of fellow decision makers that we would really rather prefer to avoid.

But I believe this is an error. I would, wouldn't I? It's the reason I am writing this book. At the same time, I hope I am making the case for why I believe this is an error, and perhaps more importantly, in the rest of the book, what we can do about it. This is about what we understand risk to be and how we approach it.

Before we do that, let us set out a vision, based on my understanding of how successful strategy making actually works in practice.

Avoid the polarizing errors

Risk is generally not overtly considered when discussing strategy, but it is implied by the approach to strategy. An interesting book by McKinsey consultant Hugh Courtney, *2020 Foresight: Crafting Strategy in an uncertain world* (2001), made a similar point when the book was published fourteen years ago, and I'm not sure we've moved that far forward since – and I wonder why not. Courtney makes the point that strategy making generally does not seem to be very good at taking account of uncertainty, and therefore working with risk. He suggests that 2020 vision is about embracing uncertainty, really understanding risk well when making strategy. I will explore more of what he proposes in Chapter 9. For now, one of his opening points is that strategists tend to have a simplistic binary view of uncertainty, either (a) we are pretty confident about the future and therefore can produce detailed plans and make investments accordingly, or (b) we have no idea, and therefore there is no point in deciding anything.

I have come to a similar conclusion in terms of how leaders think about risk, but it probably has more to do with the human psyche, intuition and character than how we might analyse and predict the future.

I believe there are two polarizing errors we encounter. The first I shall refer to as Error Type A, and is as follows:

> *Error Type A: Successful leaders take risks. I've succeeded when taking risks. Therefore take risks!*

The essence of entrepreneurship is risk taking. When we look at the likes of successful entrepreneurs such as Jobs and Gates, Branson and Dyson, what we know about them is that they took risks to establish their businesses, and we may naturally assume that risk causes success. While it is clearly a factor, a simple causal relationship is misleading. For starters, we know that for all the entrepreneurs who took risks to start businesses, there are only a few we know about because they were successful. There are many more who failed that we don't know about, and some of those probably took at least as big a risk.

In fact, the idea that 'I have taken a risk before and succeeded – therefore I will succeed when I risk again' is one of the pitfalls we describe later in Chapter 7, when I talk about cognitive inertia, and is particularly well documented in a book written by Ashridge tutors entitled *Think Again* (Campbell et al., 2008).

When thinking about this error, I am most struck by the story of the race to the South Pole by Scott and Amundsen, which Jim Collins analyses in his book, co-written with Morton Hansen, *Great by Choice* (2011). The first thing to note about the story is that both men took a big risk in choosing to try and become the first explorer to reach the South Pole. That aspect of risk was a common denominator between them – without that risk, we would not know anything about either of them.

However, this is more or less where the similarity in approach to risk stops. Collins proposes that Amundsen was more risk averse than Scott. This was in terms of the level and type or preparation before the trip, and the day-to-day decisions he took during the trip. And of the two, Amundsen was clearly the more successful, not only in terms of being the first to reach the South Pole, but on the basis that all his team survived the return trip, while none of Scott's team did.

In my own personal research of risk in leadership, I was repeatedly struck by the way leaders in high-risk roles, who accept that they deal daily with risky decisions, also describe themselves as being risk averse. I have a friend, Ian Clarke, who has taken extraordinary risks by most peoples' standards in order to set up hospitals and healthcare clinics in Uganda, amidst all the uncertainty of working in an environment that he eloquently and amusingly describes in a book he has written entitled *The Man with the Key Has Gone!* (1993). When I told him I was writing a book on risk, he was intrigued. When I asked him what his approach was to risk, his response was unequivocal: 'Avoid it at all costs!'

I describe this Error A as the Samson error. Samson had a gift of enormous strength, and he used it to great effect to take huge risks and overcome large numbers of enemy soldiers. His intuition must have told him that the key to his success was taking the risk – but in reality, the key was somewhere else, in the length of his uncut hair. When it was secretly cut, and he tried the same approach to risk, it failed him badly and he was captured.

Error Type B: The future is uncertain. Therefore don't make big choices now ... or at least be able and prepared to change them!

This is based on a view that past experience is not a sound predictor of what is to come. Our world is changing fast. New technologies are disrupting traditional ways of doing business. The internet, for example, only became a reality in the 1990s, but today with email, online buying and social media, it is an all-encompassing part of how we live and work. Any company designing a sales channel strategy in the late 1980s would probably have had to change it fairly quickly in the 1990s.

At about the same time, the Berlin Wall came down, and the communist bloc became almost instantly integrated into a global capitalist market. Russia and China have subsequently become major economic powers. Anyone formulating a global strategy in 1989 would probably have something they would want to change fairly quickly.

The current management-speak acronym for this is VUCA (which stands for Volatile, Uncertain, Complex and Ambiguous), which encapsulates the nature of the environment in which organizations need to navigate within. And to cope with this, to survive even, the established wisdom is that organizations need to be agile – that is, ready to change at the drop of a hat. This suggests that making tough, long-term, strategic choices for the future, based on market analysis, as advocated by the likes of Michael Porter, may no longer be appropriate. Apparently change is too disruptive, and accelerating at that.

The so-called 'emergent strategy' school, as pioneered by business school professor Henry Mintzberg (1994), suggests that business strategy needs to be about learning fast and adapting to the changing market – being ready to seize opportunities. Teece (2011) talks about the idea of 'dynamic capabilities', the organizational ability to sense changes in the market, to seize opportunity and change by mobilizing resource, and the ability to transform the organization to sustain the change.

This makes sense. However, the error arises when an emergent philosophy and a dynamic mindset turn into a reason not to make tough choices. This is where emergence becomes a means of avoiding risk – the risk of getting it wrong because the market has changed since we made the decision. The problem is that not making decisions that commit resources now, or that commit us to a particular message or mindset, may well lead to a lost opportunity, a loss of distinctiveness, a loss of competitive advantage or a dilution of what we are really all about.

It may appear to be lower risk to keep our options open, but lower risk often comes at a cost. If it means not being clear about our unique selling proposition (USP), or having a generic proposition which is not so unique, then customers may start to wonder what we are about, and why they should choose us. Employees may start to do the same.

If 'wait and see' means not investing in the asset or technology now, competitors may be bolder and, before we know it, we are playing cost catch-up.

When Intel invests US$5bn in a new microprocessor plant, it needs to make a tough choice. It needs a strategy that has been well analysed and thought through, and which it is prepared to stick with for a few years.

Part of the value of strategy is to be able not to react instantly to a change in circumstances, or a new opportunity – because it keeps us on track to a longer-term view of where we are going and what we are trying to achieve.

One of the most powerful uses of strategy that I have experienced is the advertising strategies that P&G attaches to its brands. A great deal of research goes into developing a new brand, and one of the outputs from this research is an advertising strategy statement, which generally sits on a single page, and describes the essence of what the brand is about. It has a standard formula that includes target audience, the core benefit offered to that audience, the all-important 'reason to believe' that the brand can deliver on that benefit, and some kind of statement of the character of the brand. This strategy statement generally stays with the brand for its life – it's the essence of what the brand is all about.

And it is used robustly with advertising agencies. These guys are paid to have the ear to the market, the latest trends and fads, what the competitors are doing, etc. And of course they are also paid to be creative. They are generally not paid, nor often particularly skilled at being strategic. That's the brand manager's role.

So when the agency presents its latest creative piece of advertising copy to the brand team, picking up on the latest market trends, the first job of the brand manager is to assess whether what has been presented is consistent with the advertising strategy for the brand. If the answer is

'No', the storyboard is rejected without any further evaluation – however brilliant it might be.

Many frustrated advertising agency executives working with P&G have experienced this rejection. Great ideas down the pan – the strategy has precedence. It works because this is fundamental to how P&G grows its business – something which it has been very good at doing for over 150 years.

A strategy needs to take the risk of carrying tough choices through the winds of change. A strategy needs to help you say 'No'. Compromising on risk and tough choices because the future is uncertain is, in my view, an error.

Choose when to risk

So to avoid these errors, effective strategic leadership is about being deliberately choiceful about risk. There is a need to sail the middle ground between the Scylla of recklessness and the Charybdis of cowardice, to take the *right* risk.

To be skilful in this is to understand the nature of risk. Effective leaders need to be effective strategists, and need to understand the nature of risk. The essence of strategy is in choosing the right risks to take.

This is as much an art as a science. We shall discover that it's about balancing an analytical and an intuitive approach. It's about being selective about information, and how we understand variability. It's about being aware of mind games and seeking to avoid psychological traps. It's about character and how that influences risk taking – it is about how organizations manifest and develop character.

Chapter 3
From strategy to character

As a strategy consultant working on a number of medium-sized businesses on making business strategy, I gradually became aware in trying to come up with useful strategies that they tended to follow common patterns. There were recurring themes on the tough questions that businesses need to ask themselves in coming up with good strategies. These themes had notable similarities with the generic strategies that Michael Porter advocated, and which I had learned at Wharton Business School. The first two of these were the need either to be the lowest cost producer in a mass market, or clearly differentiated on the basis of superior quality that customers would be prepared to pay more for. His third generic strategy was as dominant player in a focused niche market, probably through a combination of cost and quality advantage.

What I discovered when I talked to clients about these options was that they felt they could straddle different strategies, moving from one to the other either over time or in addressing different market sectors. What was also clear, however, which Porter covered to some extent, was that it was hard for organizations to sustain these different competitive positions and remain profitable. What was less clear was what aspects across the organization made this difficult to achieve.

A better answer to this question came from the work of Treacy and Wiersema in their book *The Discipline of Market Leaders* (1995), which I shall hitherto refer to as 'Treacy'. They set out three disciplines which had some resemblance to Porter's generic strategies: (a) Product Leadership, which looked a bit like the generic strategy of differentiation, (b) Operational Excellence, which looked like cost leadership, and (c) Customer Intimacy, which looked like more of a focused niche strategy.

Treacy's approach was similar to that adopted by Peters and Waterman in their book *In Search of Excellence* (1982), in which they looked at a few businesses that had definable success over a number of years, and described anecdotally what were the features of those organizations that made them successful. In contrast to Peters and Waterman's view that all their excellent companies showed strengths in a list of nine critical attributes, Treacy's hypothesis was that their businesses excelled in one, and only one, of the three disciplines. They went further than this to say that trying to excel in more than one would be a mistake, because the organizational requirements to be strong in each of the disciplines tend to create trade-offs when you compare them.

So for example, to be a product leader, you need a passion for innovation, which means you need to invest in research and development, try things and be prepared to fail, create a fairly high degree of organizational complexity as a lot of different things may be going on at the same time. To be operationally excellent, however, you need discipline in process and reduced complexity, which tends to be less forgiving of experimentation.

The conclusion I draw from the book is that business leaders need to make tough decisions as to which of the three disciplines they want to specialize in. In my experience, most leaders struggle with this idea. It is a case of taking a decision which feels somewhat risky for a couple of reasons. Firstly, because working through it would mean some aspects of the organization would need to change, and change feels risky as we move into new less well-known territory. Secondly, it feels risky because, in focusing on a single discipline, and a customer proposition based on this discipline, we hope that customers will respond better to this proposition. They may not. Or if the change means more cost, we may not be able to re-coup our costs.

They struggle with the idea that plumping for an Operational Excellence focus means the client needs to simplify process and probably cut costs. Reducing selling costs is a classic case where the proposition for customers of a more efficient lower cost operation cannot justify the cost of a field sales force. The argument is that this kind of selling can be achieved just as effectively through a call centre or online. The risk is that the client will lose sales and end up less profitable as a result.

But Treacy gives us great examples of businesses that have prospered through making tough choices, where they would have struggled if they had not. In the courier business, Fedex chose an operational excellence route through standardized processes, optimizing utilization on planes and achieving low cost advantage. Airborne Express, another courier company, chose a different customer intimate approach, setting up close partnerships with organizations like Xerox, who required highly customized service such as very early morning deliveries of parts for engineers starting their service rounds. And the point was that they would be prepared to pay more for this critical aspect of the service.

So Treacy makes a strong case for organizations focussing on one discipline, in which to excel. It made sense, and it formed the backdrop for some level of tough choices in strategy making – and choosing the right risks to take. But the question emerges: what sort of information might we need to make those kinds of tough calls? Wrestling with this question, when working with clients on strategy, led me down a path to develop a relatively simple, but I think effective, personal profiling tool.

Introducing the Blonay Profiler

I found that when I worked with clients on the organizational factors which would help inform which strategic discipline they would be most likely to prosper in, there was one important question which was hard to answer. I could see fairly readily what types of processes they had in place, how much they spent in each, what performance metrics were most important, what they told the market they were about. All of these would give me some idea of whether or not this business would lean more readily to product leading, or being intimate with customers, or being operationally excellent.

The big question I couldn't easily answer, nor could the client's senior management, was: what personal attributes of the people in the business supported one discipline or the other? So I developed a character profiling tool to help me do just that.

An important influence in developing this tool was a sentence I came across in the Apostle Paul's letter to a colleague called Timothy, for whom he was very much a mentor. Paul initially reminds him to 'fan into flame the gift that God has given him'. He is talking about personal strengths in his character. I was moved by the picture that made me think of fanning the glowing embers of a campfire to the point where it bursts into flames – the idea that a little persistent encouragement to an apparently lifeless situation with signs of potential can suddenly create so much energy and vitality. What a picture of leadership that is.

He then goes on to say, 'For God did not give us a spirit of fear, but a spirit of power, of love and of self-discipline'. I remember thinking that this sounded like a complete set of virtues to which many probably aspire and are able to exhibit to varying degrees. 'Power' spoke to me of the ability to create or inspire positive change; in other translations, it is 'boldness'. There is the virtue most closely connected with courage. This spirit is the spirit of the pioneer, bold and creative at the same time.

Then we have the spirit of love. The word 'love', I believe, is much abused in modern life to mean a plethora of things. For me, the essence is about relationship with our fellow human beings, to be committed to positive relationship. The underlying ability is to be able to see or feel things from another person's perspective: to be able to empathize.

And finally there is the spirit of self-discipline. In essence, for me, this is about a personal attention to getting and doing things right, to be ordered and organized, and to be passionately interested in truth.

These, for me, appear to be demanding personal attributes. Some of us, I suspect, are stronger in one of these virtues than in the other two. In fact, it is probably very difficult to be consistently strong in all three dimensions. Being strong in one doesn't help you to be strong in either of the other two. From a mathematical perspective, I would describe them as orthogonal – completely mutually independent of one another in terms of human character.

And it occurred to me that this was a similar story to that which Treacy tells. There are three organizational disciplines which can lead to a prosperous position in the marketplace. And it is very hard to be strong in all three because to some extent they conspire against one another. They create trade-offs. As do Paul's three virtues.

So I borrowed this idea to develop the Blonay Character Profiler, which is about assessing personal character on three character dimensions. I have called these: Bold Creative, Empathic and Self-Disciplined.

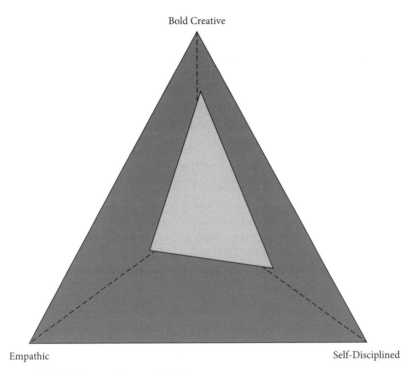

Bold Creative

Empathic   Self-Disciplined

Figure 3.1 The Blonay Character Profiler

The main similarities between these and the Treacy disciplines is the idea that these three dimensions create tensions, either within us as people, as in the case of the Character Profiler, or within organizations, as in the case of the disciplines. This means there are trade-offs to be made – dilemmas to be addressed. I have already discussed this in the organizational context, and will explain more about how this works in a personal context a bit later.

There is also some similarity in terms of what these three dimensions represent. So in this sense, I chose to map one model onto the other. Bold Creative maps to the Product Leadership discipline. Empathic maps to the Customer Intimacy discipline. And Self-Disciplined maps to the Organisational Excellence dimension.

At the time of writing, I have an as-yet unsubstantiated hypothesis that Product Leadership organizations need more Bold Creative leaders,

Customer Intimate organizations need more Empathic leaders and Operational Excellent organizations need more Self-Disciplined leaders. What I have discovered is that the Blonay model has a high level of resonance with managers considering these kinds of issues, more generally in connection with strategy. The model also works well in helping to understand the attitude and appetite that individuals have towards risk. Bold Creatives tend to have a greater appetite for risk than the other two character attributes.

Before developing the dynamics of this profiler further, I was further encouraged in my quest to focus on these three character attributes by the work of Jim Collins at Stanford, covered in his book *Good to Great* (2001). Jim Collins in his research identified that the leadership characteristics which differentiated his high-flying eleven organizations from the rest seem to fall into three buckets: discipline, humility and resolve. The Blonay Profiler mirrors these in a similar set of three character attributes.

Modelling character tensions

So the Blonay Profiler provides a way of assessing character bias based on these three dimensions

1. **BOLD CREATIVE** – Those with a Bold Creative bias will have an above-average appetite for positive risk taking, with an interest in innovation and change. They prefer to be proactive, and tend to have a preference for informal intuitive thinking over more formal analytical process. They can be seen as pioneers, and will have a track record of starting things. They have antennae that look out from themselves and often from the organization. Because they tend to challenge the status quo, they can find themselves isolated in organizations.

2. **EMPATHIC** – Those with an Empathic bias place a priority on understanding and working with people, on building relationships. They prefer to respond to situations rather than take a proactive stance. They tend to be more tuned to emotions and can be quite sensitive. They often have a keen sense of mercy, and are most ready

to forgive the shortcomings of others. They tend to look out from themselves to others.

3. **SELF-DISCIPLINED** – Those with a Self-Disciplined bias are more concerned than others about doing the right things and in the right way. They tend to prefer formal process and structure to informality. They are often analytical, logical, numerical, data driven, and have a high sense of truth, integrity and justice. They tend also to be more inward looking to themselves, and to understanding the world from their own perspective.

Those of you who are familiar with different psychometric tools will see similarities with these instruments, which are generally used to help build self-awareness. For example, the Strength Deployment Inventory (SDI) is a psychometric tool that is used extensively with programme participants at Ashridge to build self-awareness and help develop relational effectiveness. The main tool is based on a colour-coded triangular mapping approach, similar to the Blonay Profiler. The colours used are blue, red and green. Blue is defined as Altruistic-Nurturing, and could be compared to the Empathic dimension on the Profiler. Green is Analytic-Autonomizing and could be compared to Blonay's Self-Disciplined dimension. The least good fit, although there are some similarities, is the red dimension in the SDI tool, which is defined as Assertive Directing, whereas the Character Profiler has a Bold Creative dimension.

The Profiler is based on a set of 'character' tensions that manifest themselves when faced with dilemmas as to how to behave in different situations. And it is designed to help individuals and groups work with dilemmas more effectively, by understanding better their own character biases, as well as those of others. These tensions are understood by looking in turn at each of the sides of the Blonay Profiler triangle, as shown in the diagram below. The tensions are represented by the differences between each of the triangle apexes on the side being explored. So to illustrate, let us look at each of the sides in turn.

'Bold Creative' versus 'Self-Disciplined'

The 'Bold Creative' versus 'Self-Disciplined' dimension reflects the tensions between informal and formal aspects of organizational life – the tensions between celebrating diversity and the need for

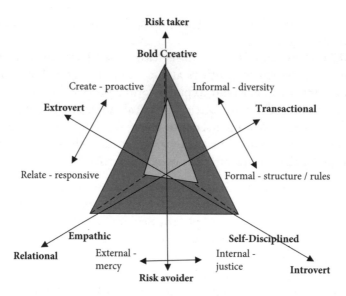

Figure 3.2 The tensions between the dimensions.

some level of rules-based process for an organization or community to be able to function.

For example, leaders in creative and professional services firms regularly face this dilemma, often referred to as the challenge of 'herding cats'. 'Bold Creative' behaviour by professionals, shown as being prepared to challenge and bringing innovation, and having different individual ways of addressing issues, is important for the ongoing success of these firms. But these don't necessarily lead to the most efficient way to run the organization. Leaders who seek to impose a more Self-Disciplined, process-oriented approach to drive greater efficiency will risk undermining the 'Bold Creative' attributes of the organization.

'Empathic' versus 'Self-Disciplined'

On the 'Empathic' versus 'Self-Disciplined' axis, we pick up the tension between an external people-oriented view and an internal data-driven view. This has resonance with one of the oldest dilemmas of all – that of mercy versus justice, mercy being the 'Empathic' option and justice being the 'Self-Disciplined' one.

This relates to another typical dilemma faced by business leaders. You have collected and analysed cost and performance data which indicates that making certain people redundant is the right decision for the business. However, this would have severe consequences for the people and potentially the local community where they work. Do you proceed? The 'Self-Disciplined' approach suggests that you do; the 'Empathic' approach suggests you think again.

'Bold Creative' versus 'Empathic'

Finally, the trade-off between 'Bold Creative' and 'Empathic' can be characterized as a trade-off between taking a higher risk proactive approach or a more collaborative, listening, responsive approach. This links with classic theory on innovation: does it come from 'inspired' Bold Creative moves or more from being better at listening and responding to customers? Was the real drive behind innovation at organizations like Apple, Facebook and Google listening better to what customers said they wanted, or bold initiatives by entrepreneurs who were prepared to buck the trend and established wisdom?

A personal profile, on these three character dimensions, can be scored by completing an electronic self-completion questionnaire of twenty-one multiple choice questions, based on regular day-to-day situations requiring choices. The questions are based on selecting a likely preferred behaviour in a range of scenarios. Respondents choose from a range of four options for each scenario; but each scenario effectively addresses one of the three sets of tensions described above.

Organizational character at the heart of strategy

If we wind back the logic clock on our model of character, we remember that we got here by considering what generic strategies or disciplines organizations need to be effective. And I have sought to argue that there is a direct mapping between those disciplines and individual character attributes.

So part of what we have here is a picture of organizational character at the heart of strategy. In making strategic decisions, we are asking to what extent do we bring a Bold Creative approach to this need or opportunity. To what extent do we bring an Empathic approach? To what extent is this about our ability to practise our Self-Discipline? So I would argue that the degree to which we have a Bold Creative character as an organization is the extent to which we are comfortable with risk taking; it is a measure of the organization's risk appetite.

In contrast, the level to which we look to an Empathic response corresponds to our organizational bias to employ a relational approach. This becomes one way we tend to avoid risk, or mitigate it.

Likewise, if Self-Disciplined is at the heart of our organizational character, then we would look to analytical rigour and defined process as a way to reduce the risk or pursuing an opportunity or addressing an issue.

To give an example of this, I have been involved in developing strategy for Ashridge Business School. When we think about our competitive position in the international markets in which we compete, a stand-out characteristic of what we do which appears as one of our strengths is the level of focus we place on customizing or adapting executive education programmes to the needs of corporate customers. While other major international business schools offer customized executive education programmes, the proportion of standardized to customized programmes tends to be a lot higher than is the case for Ashridge. And this is reflected on the way our world rankings are measured – we have historically been scored high on our ability to customize.

So we appear superficially to be good in this area. Is this an accident of circumstance, or just the way we have developed our reputation over the years? Or is there more to this? As it happens, as a group of us have been developing our 'risk' proposition, I have also had a sample of staff at Ashridge complete the Blonay Profiler questionnaire. Overall, the proportion of people from a smattering of different organizations who have completed the questionnaire with a bias in any of the three attributes is equally distributed – almost exactly a third, a third, a third. But in the case of Ashridge, a much higher proportion has an Empathic bias (37%). This is confirmed by my own experience of the character of my colleagues. I believe there is a case for saying that Ashridge has an Empathic organizational character, and that this has to influence strategic decision making.

Is this any different from saying that Customer Intimacy is Ashridge's preferred discipline? There is a case for this, but it's interesting to observe that not everything that Ashridge does demonstrates high levels of Customer Intimacy. For example, our processes don't really support this. So I believe there is a difference.

Another example perhaps makes this point more clearly. Procter & Gamble (P&G), my former employer, is held up as a good example of Product Leadership. It is a stated part of P&G's strategy to become leaders in the consumer product categories in which they compete. And they achieve this through product innovation, continually launching new products with, as they call it, 'big edge' quality advantages over competition, often these days on a global scale. So this would suggest, according to my analysis, an organizational character of the Bold Creative.

But when you look further at how they achieve these successes, we notice perhaps another aspect to the character, an aspect which I recall only too well during my time there learning how to be a good marketeer.

Part of their strategy is based on a strength they call their 'Go to market' capability. What is this? Essentially this is the way they are confident that when they come to launch a product globally, or even at an individual country level, it will be successful. It's all about consumer research and market testing. They follow strict disciplines, based on years of experience. The organizational character, I believe, is much more akin to Self-Disciplined. It permeates every part of the company. You can see it in their obsession with integrity; sometimes you would argue boringly so. How products are marketed? How people are treated? You see the discipline to extreme even in how documents are written and agreement is reached. It is the character that was formed, probably by the founders, Procter and Gamble themselves, who started with an obsession to make soap and candles to rigid levels of quality, and make sure customers were not cheated in any way.

I will talk more about how risk features in strategy in P&G in Chapter 8, when we consider that the concept of 'winning' is at the heart of what makes strategy risky.

For now, I leave this section having planted the idea that organizational character is at the heart of strategy. We will see in this as we go through how this can have an impact on how we work with risk in making strategic decisions.

We now take a different tack, and look at how a specific issue that we have been researching at Ashridge, that of modern slavery, demonstrates how organizational character impacts the approach to risk and strategy amongst a smattering of the UK's largest and best known retail branded organizations.

Researching modern slavery

Slavery has been a feature of humanity throughout most of recorded history. From the early days of global trade until the early nineteenth century, trade in slave labour was a common part of the world's commercial landscape. Most would think that slavery was no longer a feature of our world, after it was abolished. This is not the case – it still exists. The term used to describe it is 'modern slavery', which encompasses slavery, servitude, forced and compulsory labour and human trafficking. Various official bodies estimate the extent of modern slavery as being between 21 and 36 million people globally (Lake et al., 2015).

The Modern Slavery Act was passed into British law on 26 March 2015, and requires about 12,000 businesses in the UK to disclose each year what action they have taken to ensure there is no modern slavery in their business or supply chains.

Ashridge teamed up with a London-based charitable organization called the Ethical Trading Initiative to conduct research into how businesses were dealing with the issue of modern slavery in the supply chain (Lake et al., 2015). My colleague Quintin Lake was the main driving force behind the research, and as a specialist in the subject, wanted the research to help businesses learn from each other to find the most effective way of tackling the issue. I joined the team doing the research, as I was particularly interested in how risk played out in tackling this issue. I also wanted to explore how strategic this issue was, and how leaders generally were dealing with possible trade-offs and dilemmas relating to addressing ethical trade and workers' rights in the supply chain more broadly.

We are arguably most aware of risk when faced with dilemmas – decisions typically carrying two options, both of which hold some element of risk. And these dilemmas can be the most difficult to address where they carry an ethical dimension, which they often do. They become more difficult because they require a deeper level of understanding between the members of top teams. Ethical perspectives can be very personal, and at the same time very personally important – and can differ significantly across leadership teams.

My hypothesis in starting the research was that the issue of modern slavery presents a significant strategic dilemma for the top teams of some organizations. Our research confirmed that this kind of slavery is likely to be present in the early stages of the supply chains of most major global organizations. These organizations are engaged in strategies which involve a significant amount of risk in bringing new high volume products to market, at low cost, and with the optimal ability to adapt to changes in the market as quickly as possible. An effective global supply chain is a critical success factor in being able to do this in a highly competitive market. So the risk of unearthing and addressing the possibility of slavery in the supply chain is potentially high, particularly if competitors don't follow suit. But the risk of this becoming a major reputational issue is also high. This echoes one of the themes from the initial Ashridge research into risk: 'Risk if you do, risk if you don't!'

The impact of major UK retail brands

In the research, we talked to senior managers responsible for ethical trade, and in some cases corporate social responsibility, in many of the main retailers in the UK, particularly in the food and clothing sectors. A number of the ethical supply chain issues that have been reported by the media in recent months have come from those sectors.

These conversations confirmed that risk, and specifically reputational risk, was an important factor in the way these organizations were tackling modern slavery. The use of the word 'slavery' in the debates around the UK Modern Slavery Act 2015 has led to a higher level of engagement with the issue amongst managers, something which less emotive terms like 'human rights' or 'workers' right' have not achieved. This has all happened at a time when concerns about migration into Europe, and thence into the UK, are also growing.

What has been less clear so far from these conversations is that managers are concerned about the risks of disruption to the supply chain in tackling this issue – at least not from the people we were speaking to. We also do not yet get the sense that this is being tackled as a strategic issue, even though clearly the global supply chain is a significant source of competitive advantage. In fact, there is a clear sense that this issue should not be tackled from a competitive perspective, but very much from a collaborative perspective.

The story that has emerged from this research is that collaboration of major UK retail brands can have influence to bring about significant change in workers' rights, not only in developing countries but also in the developed economies. These issues are increasingly turning up in our own backyard. It's bad news that it's happening here. It's good news that we can learn from how to tackle the issue in other countries.

I believe our research into how UK retail brands are tackling the issue of modern slavery is a great backdrop story to the way I propose we should think differently about making strategy, and the extent to which risk plays a role in that. So throughout the book I shall be referring back to some of the things we have learned in this research.

Chapter 4

Understanding risk

Having set out the case that risk should be central to strategy making, I think it's useful to take a closer look at the nature of risk. How we define it is key to how we work with it, so let's start there.

In a fascinating paper 'The Etymology of Risk', Cline (2004) argues that there is no consistent definition of risk, that as a concept it is unstable and that the meaning of risk has evolved over time. In history, it is shrouded in mythology, associated with philosophy and religion – 'the domain of the gods'. At one point, the character of risk was considered more important than the outcome. Taking a risk was often considered a virtue and associated with courage. Only in more recent times has the avoidance of risk, encapsulated in the word 'prudence', been also seen as a virtue. The idea that risk can be measured appeared with the arrival of probability theory, and the work of Blaise Pascal in the seventeenth century, born through the study of gambling. Since then, it has become 'Janus-faced', with one side statistical and the other based on belief.

We have noticed that people refer to it a lot in conversation, but it means different things in different contexts. Sometimes when we talk about it, for example, our emphasis is on avoiding danger or harm. At other times, it's more to do with seizing opportunity. The Chinese appear to be more overt about this and denote the closest concept to our word risk, which also signifies crisis, in two separate characters: one denoting danger and the other denoting opportunity.

One of the observations that prompted our research project on how leaders work with risk was noticing that ours and other business school texts seem to focus on the danger aspect of risk, and describe processes for 'managing risk' that can also be described as driving risk out. They would be asking things like: 'What are the risks?' and 'How do we minimize them?'

This seemed at odds with the approach other leaders took, in talking about risk in terms of opportunity. They typically ask questions like: 'Shall we take the risk?'

Danger   Opportunity

Figure 4.1 Chinese for risk or crisis

This bi-modal theme carried into other aspects of risk: a more analytical mathematical approach playing against a more intuitive psychological approach.

The psychology of definition

Psychologists tell us that meaning is a fundamental driver of behaviour. That's why what we mean by 'risk' is so important.

Probably the most common definition of risk is as a measure of both the likelihood and impact of something happening which can cause harm. In fact, most formal risk management approaches in the organizations I have encountered would tend to work with something like this definition of risk. This creates the impression first that risk is primarily something negative, and therefore something we need to reduce or avoid. It colludes with a psychological phenomenon known as 'loss aversion', which I shall go into in greater depth later on. The idea is that when considering the likelihood of a range of possible future outcomes of an action we might take, we tend not to treat downside and upside potential in a symmetrical way. We are more concerned with what we could lose, rather than being positive about what we could gain. So risk management, where risk is defined in this way, colludes with our disproportionate desire to minimize the chance of bad news.

Another aspect of this definition of risk is that it is measurable. This clearly encourages us to look for ways to measure likelihood and impact of possible outcomes, which generally means we need to seek more and better information, and better ways of analysing that information. This is a good thing as far as it goes. However, what it tends to diminish in terms of behaviour is valuing the aspects of decision making that are not based on overt or objective information: intuition and emotion. It also implies that aspects of decisions and possible outcomes that are not readily measurable must fall outside the scope of risk management. So we can end up with an almost schizophrenic way of looking at our future: aspects which are measurable, which come under risk management, and aspects which are not, which need to be dealt with in a different way. Then I think we can lose some of the richness of a more holistic way of looking at decisions and outcomes.

However, when we look at how the word 'risk' is used more generally, as already discussed, aspects such as 'opportunity' and 'intuition' are thrown into the mix. These are generally not included in risk management thinking, but they inevitably form part of management thinking. I would argue they could add a richness to the way we view risk management, a subject which I believe most managers tackle reluctantly as a necessary evil – because it's all about the prospect of bad news and is for specialists who understand numbers.

Some might argue that these more 'colloquial' ways of defining and thinking about risk are not the real thing. They are just expressions that are hangovers from the ancient ways of seeing risk, as something heroic and instinctive, but with no real value in today's more scientifically minded commercial world. But on further examination, this clearly isn't true. In fact, probably the most common use of the word 'risk' in commercial decision making is highly scientific. And while it is defined in terms of measurability, it is not focused on avoiding hazard and harm. It is viewed primarily as 'variability' and used extensively in financial analysis.

Risk as variability

Financial analysts define risk as variability. The implication is that the emphasis is on the downside, but in reality there is upside as well as downside. There is an assumption in financial risk that upside and downside probabilities and impacts are symmetrical. Typically, financial analysts are interested in return on investment (ROI), and for any prospective decision to invest, whether it be in shares in a company or a quantity of a commodity, they are looking to predict the most likely return on that investment. They also recognize that they are unlikely to predict that return perfectly, so they are also interested in the range of returns that are likely to result from that investment. They typically refer to the range of possible outcomes above a certain level of likelihood as the risk associated with that investment.

This variability of likely outcomes can be represented by normal curves as shown in the diagrams below (Figure 4.2). This curve shows on the horizontal x-axis the range of possible outcomes from a decision, and on the vertical y-axis the likelihood of each of those outcomes occurring. The peak of the normal curve coincides with what is known as the expected outcome – the most likely outcome to occur on the x-axis. A measure of the range of likely outcomes in the case of a normal curve pattern is the standard deviation – this is a measure of the difference in outcome between the expected outcome, the x value associated with the peak of the curve, and either a poorer or better outcome with a defined level of likelihood of occurrence. It's the same number for either poorer or better outcomes because the curve is symmetrical.

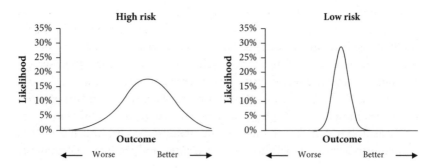

Figure 4.2 Risk as statistical variability

So in the case of a decision that has a wide range of possible outcomes, that is, high variability, we would consider this high risk. This is represented by the normal curve on the left, which shows that a wider range of possible outcomes has a reasonable likelihood, whereas in a situation where there is less uncertainty, the range of possible outcomes is smaller, and we have a lower risk decision as represented by the curve on the right. Our expected outcome is more likely to occur, and wide variations from this outcome have very low likelihood.

So to conclude, when we see risk as variability, one way to represent this is by the broadness or pointedness of a normal curve, plotting the percentage likelihood (y-axis) of different possible outcomes (x-axis).

Risk as crisis – a public management view

In other circles of life, risk is more generally associated with crisis. It's about the impact and likelihood of something particularly harmful or damaging happening. When we consider risk in this way, it is generally not associated with a range of possible outcomes, symmetrically distributed around an expected outcome. It is generally an evaluation of a single bad outcome, which is very different from the expected outcome, which is often the status quo.

While risk as variability is the common view of measures of financial performance in competitive businesses, the risk as crisis view is more common in the public sector, and is very much at the heart of the business model of insurance companies. The prevailing wisdom is that this kind of crisis risk needs to be minimized wherever possible – which is not necessarily the case for risk as variability.

So it was with some interest that I recently read a report by the UK Government Office for Science (Peplow, 2014), which is entitled 'Innovation: Managing Risk, Not Avoiding it'. It's interesting because while innovation in the business marketplace is seen as risky because it can deliver a range of possible outcomes from very good to very poor (i.e. risk as variability), in the realm of public management it's about how to encourage innovation that doesn't lead to crisis of some kind or another. The report covers case studies of earthquakes, contagious disease, deliberate or accidental nuclear explosions, unintended consequences of new technology like genetics, a catastrophic computer virus and even the financial crisis.

This is clearly a very different view of risk.

The common denominator that makes this broad exploration of risk definition enlightening is the underlying variables which can lead either to a range of possible outcomes (risk as variability) or a particular extreme unwanted outcome (risk as crisis).

Understanding variables

In fact, the same variables have an impact on either view of risk, clearly to different degrees.

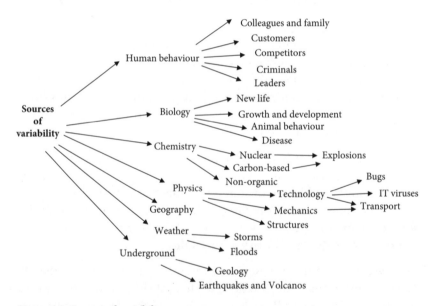

Figure 4.3 Sources of variability

In the chart above (Figure 4.3), I have listed various sources of variability that have an impact on our view of risk. Some are more likely to relate to a typical business view of risk as variability; others more likely to feature in a public management view of risk in terms of crisis.

For many businesses, the variability of customer behaviour has a significant impact on business risk; but likewise, the variability of the behaviour of colleagues in our same business can impact risk, as can other factors outside our control: weather, unexpected technology variations, etc.

These sources of variability relate to von Clausewitz's (1976) sources of friction, which are adapted by my colleague Stephen Bungay (2011) to bring it into a business context. Bungay builds on von Clausewitz's views on implementing strategy to develop the case for why strategies fail to get implemented effectively in business. The sources of friction are indeed some of the key variables listed above: (1) the behaviours of colleagues in your organization, and the extent to which they behave in line with the strategy; (2) the behaviour of competitors (or enemy leaders, as Clausewitz viewed it) who are likely to be doing whatever they can to stop the strategy being effective; and (3) there are what Clausewitz calls external events – these can be weather, geography or all manner of non-controllable variables that can get in the way.

When we look at these in the context of crisis, while some have an obvious link (floods, explosions, disease, etc.), the more compelling analysis is to consider the combinations of some of these variables: for example, 'criminals' combined with 'IT viruses', or, 'leaders' combined with 'nuclear weapons'. Theses are at the heart of the existential risks that are considered in the *Government Office for Science Report* (Peplow, 2014).

Risk as cause and effect

One of the other ways in which the word 'risk' is used differently is in defining categories of risk (see Figure 4.4). Typically, this categorization of risk throws up a mix of possible causes of variable outcomes, or the outcomes themselves, that is, the effects. And sometimes our categorization straddles the two, or can indeed be both.

So for example, when we talk about fire risk or health risk, we are generally talking about an outcome – the likelihood and impact of there being a fire or damage to health. When we talk about market risk or supply chain risk, we are generally talking about a cause – the variability of behaviour inherent in the market or the supply chain that can then create problems for our business financial performance, which we may then refer to as a financial risk, or an effect.

During our research on modern slavery, I have found it quite enlightening to ask respondents to be more specific about what they mean when they talk about assessing risk in the supply chain. What they typically mean is the risk of discovering some kind of problem in the supply chain – this is really a cause. When I ask them to expand on what they mean in terms of the harm caused, I got a range of responses from risk to the health of the workers concerned, to the reputational risk to the business if this problem is picked up in the media, to even the legal risk, the possibility of being sued.

All of this points to a reality that we should not make assumptions that we know what people mean when they talk about risk.

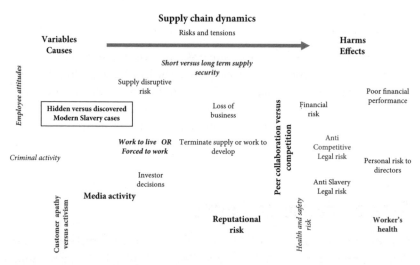

Figure 4.4 Categorizing risk

Whose risk is it?

Our modern slavery research respondents talked to us variously about reputational risk, and risk to the workers' health. This raises another important difference in the way people think about risk. Generally, when we talk about risk in this formal sense, we are talking about risk to the organization or community. But in other situations, what we are really considering is personal individual risk – often risk to ourselves.

There are clearly similarities – we would probably think of risk of fire or theft in a similar way, whether we are looking at this at a personal level or a corporate level. But in some situations, the interpretation of risk as either corporate or personal can lead us down very different paths.

In the area of strategic decision making, this is a very real issue. When we talk about a risky decision, are we talking about risk to the individual taking the decision, or to the business about which the decision has been taken?

I explore this factor in more depth in subsequent chapters on both how leaders actually work with risk and, in coming to terms with the agency problem, the issue raised by personal and organizational risks not being aligned, which I explore more in Chapter 12.

Risk plays uncertainty

Frank Knight, an economist in the early twentieth century (1921), is well known, amongst economists at least, for drawing a clear distinction between the concepts of risk and uncertainty. Essentially, he argues that risk is measurable or at least quantifiable, whereas uncertainty is not. He illustrated this by imagining an opaque linen bag of coloured balls, and an exercise of hand picking a ball out of the bag at random. The likelihood of picking a red ball out of the bag would be a case of dealing with risk, if you know in advance what proportion of the balls in the bag were red. If you didn't know what proportion of the balls in the bag were red, then you were dealing with uncertainty. After all, there may be no red balls in the bag, or they may all be red.

This is a distinction that many economists and business planners still work with today. Another more trendy version of this distinction is the distinction between 'known unknowns' (risk) and 'unknown unknowns' (uncertainty) as popularized by the US Senator Donald Rumsfeld in connection with the Iraq conflict and the question of the existence of weapons of mass destruction.

While it is indeed an interesting distinction, for me it is unhelpful on a couple of counts. Firstly, it suggests that our ability to forecast is a binary issue: the likelihood that something will happen is either quantifiable or it isn't. This clearly isn't the case – there are various degrees of quantifiability. So to pick up on Knight's coloured balls in an opaque bag example, what if we have already selected some balls at random and they have all so far turned out to be red? Or we have received an unconfirmed report from several people who have seen the balls that they are all red? Or we have been told that there is a 50 per cent probability that all the balls are red? None of these bits of information give us a sound basis for calculating the probability of picking a red ball, but they all give us some basis for estimating its likelihood. So, is this risk or uncertainty?

We also know that the history of the word 'risk' was more about courage and daring, generally in the face of uncertainty, long before it became associated with probability. We use the word colloquially to mean not only some uncertain sense of danger, but also an instinctive sense of opportunity and venture. This brings a richness to the word which I believe we miss when we delegate it solely to the domain of the mathematicians and financial analysts. I hope to be able to demonstrate this richness in this book.

It's the ambivalence in the definition of the word 'risk' that in my view gives it its heart. It is itself a courageous word because it dares to defy precise definition. Let's expand on how we can benefit from that by exploring further what came out of our research, in terms of how leaders work with risk.

Working with risk – Ashridge research

In 2012, I joined a research team at Ashridge that set out to understand better how organizational leaders work with risk (West et al., 2014). Ashridge has a rich tradition in Executive Education, and specializes in strategy, leadership and organization. We knew that leaders were interested in the topic or risk, but they told us that what business schools offered was insufficient to help them deal with the dilemmas they encountered daily.

There is plenty of business literature on the subject of risk. Attempts to quantify risk were made as early as the mid-seventeenth century by

Blaise Pascal (Ross, 2004). However, there is relatively little research on the practicalities of how leaders work with risk on a day-to-day basis. There seems to be a paradox – as argued by some of our participants, risk seems to be a central part of leadership.

Yet in most of today's organizations, risk is the domain of the finance department, overseen by a risk committee consisting mainly of non-executive directors – or a specialized risk department. It may be delegated to special processes and documentation – risk assessments and risk registers. Or it may even be outsourced to specialist organizations – insurance, regulators, etc. – sometimes supported by sophisticated mathematical models.

In our research, we conducted semi-structured interviews with senior managers, trying to understand better how they think about and work with risk. The study covered thirty-four managers who were risk specialists and/or organizational leaders from a comprehensive range of industry sectors, including healthcare, finance, legal, manufacturing, technology, housing, insurance and IT.

The interviews had the following five sections:

- 'You and your role'
- 'How you think about risk, in principle?'
- 'How you work with risk, in practice?'
- 'What stories do you have about working with risk, both good and bad?'
- 'What better would look like' in terms of thinking about and working with risk?

All interviews were transcribed and analysed to identify common themes. From these themes, it was possible to identify the different ways that risk is dealt with in principle and in practice, as well as the challenges these bring. The implications for managers in general were developed following this analysis.

Our research concluded with the following **eight Pointers**:

1. People define and see risk in different ways – understand difference and establish common ground!
2. There are formal/analytical and informal/intuitive approaches to working with risk – work with both!

3. Each approach can create or be based on 'illusion' – check for this!
4. Principles and values impact how managers work with risk (and vice versa).
5. Consider both individual and collective accountability for risk – align them!
6. Risk is associated with change – consider the risk of not changing!
7. Leaders need to recognize that risk is their 'job calling'.
8. Consider a culture that encourages conversations about risk.

I have already covered Pointer 1, concerning definition, in the lead up to this chapter. And I am just about to elaborate on Pointer 2, formal and informal approaches, in the next section, by introducing you to tigers and elephants, who are central characters in this risk story.

I dedicate another section of this book to unpacking the issue of illusions and traps (Pointer 3) that managers can get caught in when considering risk. For this, I draw from and attempt to summarize some of the concepts highlighted by few pioneers of this subject, including Nassim Taleb and Daniel Kahneman. My colleagues at the Ashridge Strategic Management also significantly contributed to this subject in their book *Think Again* (Campbell et al., 2008).

As for the last five Pointers, I will cover these in the latter half of this book, when I explore the subject of organizational character. Extending the idea that organizations need to be aligned around strategy, I am particularly interested in the idea of organizational character, and how this can lead to risk in strategy while it needs to support it. In fact, I believe effective strategies are generally imbued with a sense of organizational character. As part of this character, principles and values (Pointer 4) can have a huge impact on how leaders work with risk, specifically personal risk. A principle-based decision is often a tough decision – tough because there is implicit risk in it.

Change in organizations means taking risk (Pointer 6). There is a risk in innovating, which means trying new things or moving into new areas that we know less about, so there is more uncertainty. There is an aspect of organizational character that makes this more likely to take place or even encourages it to happen. The opposite is true for organizations that don't have this aspect of character.

Organizational culture is a clue to the character of the organization. So we are looking for a culture that encourages conversations about risk, or that encourages risky conversations (Pointer 8). It's the same kind of culture that is open to failure, because increased risk probably means an increased likelihood of failure. It's a culture that accepts imperfection as the price of being comfortable with risk. As a result, it is more or less ready to face the uncertainty of the future, because paradoxically there is risk in not changing, not innovating or not addressing the possibility of failure. There is, in fact, risk in 'not risking'.

We shall briefly explore Taleb's world of anti-fragility (*Antifragile – How to Live in a World We Don't Understand*, 2012), which works to embrace failure, rather than shun it, in order to create new success. Because that's the way our world seems to work – the branch is pruned and new life emerges.

Part of the story is accountability (Pointer 5) and ensuring it is aligned, which is part of anti-fragility – making sure there is 'skin in the game' for the decision makers.

And yes, this is all 'Job 1' for leadership (Pointer 7), whose approach to risk in decision making sets the tone for organizational character. The Blonay Character Profiler is a starting point for understanding the different character attributes of leaders, and how this is reflected in the rest of the organization.

Tigers and elephants

One of our respondents pointed out that the reason for the success of a major global product launch was the presence of a combination of 'elephants' and 'tigers' in the launch team. This technical product needed to be developed quickly but also reliably, to seize an important opportunity in a fast growing consumer electronics market. In essence, this respondent described these two types of individuals involved in the launch process as follows:

Elephants are methodical and analytical, have good memories, build momentum, but tend to be slow and grey. They are the formal risk

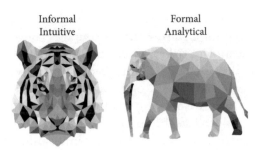

Informal
Intuitive

Formal
Analytical

Figure 4.5 Tigers and elephants

workers who assessed risk using objective, quantifiable and evidence-based outputs. Often working in response to regulation (compliance, governance, legal, industry standardization), their focus was on high visual sharpness, accuracy and timeliness in an attempt to reduce subjectivity.

Tigers are colourful, fast, intuitive and brave, but if you have too many, you have chaos. They are the informal risk workers who use peripheral vision to scan the environment and to provide space for generating hypotheses. Sometimes referred to as instinct, gut feel or common sense, this requires an inherent ability to consider what is at stake by looking for threat or identifying opportunity. There is no single focus of informal risk; 'three-dimensional', 'entrepreneurial', 'holistic' and 'peripheral vision' are the words we heard managers use when describing how informal risk perceivers scan their environment.

> *We needed to manage the speed and still have control and manage the risk. We used the approach called Tigers and Elephants. You can have one tiger in the one forest and he can manage, but if you have too many tigers, it will be chaos. We need elephants to deliver good basic policies and structure. But when you need to get something done fast or make something that is creative, then you need a tiger. The connotation for both words are good (sic): the elephants are big, they are strong, and they are long-timers with experience, wisdom and long memories. The tigers are flexible, driven by speed, they are hunters who deliver quickly and decisively.*
>
> *Ashridge research interviewee quote*

As we reviewed the responses from our leaders on how they tended to work with risk, it became clear that there were broadly two ways in which they engaged with it.

There was a formal way, which was all about analysis, risk assessment, and processes and models. These were designed to work out what kinds of risks were likely to happen, when based on some kind of evidence, and what we can do to reduce the likelihood of a harmful outcome.

The second way was the informal way. This was much more about working with risk in an intuitive manner. These leaders are aware of risk being around them daily, and that many of the decisions that they make daily have a distinct risk element to them. And the decisions they made would be based on some kind of judgements about that risk, with very little overt evidence.

It struck us that the elephant and tiger picture language that our respondent used to illustrate this particular case was a great way of describing these two modes for working with risk. The elephants are the ones who work with risk in a formal analytical way, and the tigers are the ones who work with risk in an informal, intuitive way.

We had the sense that while circumstances may well dictate in which of these two modes risk thinking is most comfortable, it seemed clear that some people prefer the formal, elephant approach, and believe that is the only way to think about risk. In fact, going back to our debate around Knightian definition, they would probably say if you can't deal with risk in this way, then it's not risk, it's uncertainty – and that's something different altogether.

Other people prefer a more informal, intuitive way of thinking about risk. They may also call it uncertainty. But they say things like 'I feel comfortable taking the risk', or 'For me, the risk is acceptable'. It's a personal assessment, with no overt data. In fact, I would say that it's this personal fingerprint on the assessment of risk that is a defining characteristic of leadership.

Fast and slow thinking

The idea of the two modes of working with risk is not new. Glynis Breakwell explores a similar theme in *The Psychology of Risk* (2014). She talks about the 'dual processing' model: one process is embedded in an intuitive, experiential, affective base, while the other embedded in formal, propositional, information-processing base.

There is particular resonance with Kahneman's explanation of System 1 and System 2 thinking, as explored in his book *Thinking, Fast and Slow* (Kahneman 2011). There are some interesting differences in emphasis though. Kahneman notes that we all have a tendency for both fast, intuitive System 1 thinking and slow, rational System 2 thinking, and suggests that while we should pay attention to both, we need to be cautious about the priority we give to the faster thinking. This is because of the logical or psychological traps that we can fall into with System 1 thinking.

Our research, in describing tigers (System 1) and elephants (System 2), highlighted the fact that organizations can have different individuals who have a preference to work in one mode or the other. We also observed that leaders can tend to have this same preference, and as a result, can either not be aware of or ignore the other mode.

Our argument is that this is a mistake. We say that leaders and the organizations that they lead will benefit by paying attention to both modes. Both modes bring benefits: working exclusively in one mode can fall prey to unhelpful illusions and biases.

And we would say the same about those modes of thinking within individual human beings. There may be a preference for one mode or the other, but pay attention to the unpreferred mode. When we explore great strategic decision making, we observe that those decisions are made to operate in both modes.

Most of our respondents tended to think of risk in one or other of these modes. There are pros and cons of each. The cons are that both are susceptible to illusions and traps, some of which I describe in Chapter 7. Both also have strengths and can complement each other. While individuals may have a preference to operate in one mode or the other, some are comfortable operating in both modes.

So our conclusion in the Ashridge research was that you need both. Later in the book, I will give examples of effective strategic leadership based on combining both.

In the meantime, let's look at each in turn.

Chapter 5

Elephants and formal risk management

Firstly, let's explore a little more about the 'elephant' formal view of risk – this is the one that is more commonly discussed in textbooks, and often views risk as something dangerous and at the very least, something to be managed, if not driven out.

Elephants generally try to make risk measurable in some way, even when the evidence to support the measures may be quite subjective and not particularly strong. They would argue that some measure is better than none.

They often define risk as an equation something like this: risk factor = impact factor × likelihood of occurrence. At one level, they may be able to turn this into a financial view. Risk (£) = expected impact (£) × probability (%), and would relate it to a particular time period, say a year, and impact perhaps on costs or profits. Where it is just a factor, without defined units, what is important is that the factor is calculated consistently for different situations, options, scenarios, etc., so that they can be compared.

So for example, in the risk analysis associated with modern slavery, the risk factors are calculated by audit firms who use common approaches for different clients and suppliers to make them comparable. The probability factor calculations are based on a series of tell-tale signs, which they know from experience suggest the existence of a problem with various degrees of likelihood. The country in which the audit is taking place will also lead to another factor being applied, again based on experience of the frequency of occurrence of problems in that country. And the impact factor is yet another calculation, which includes the amount of trade being done with that supplier.

In addition to clarifying the basis of measurement, elephants also typically categorize risk. This is to break the analysis down into manageable chunks, and make it clearer what to do about it. This is where they can run into problems in mixing up causes (e.g. market risk) with effects (e.g. financial risk). One of the problems here is that you can end up double counting your risk.

Formal risk management practice

1. Categorize risk
2. Analyse scenarios and score risks
3. Prioritize and mitigate risk
4. Plan contingencies

Assuming they don't do that, elephants can end up with a list of risk categories, perhaps in a range of different situations or scenarios, with some kind of risk score associated with each. Then, assuming we are focusing on the downside in our risk measure, they will look to mitigate the risk. They look to find ways to reduce either the likelihood of the risk being realized, and/or the impact it can have if it is realized.

Smart elephants differentiate between risk mitigation and contingency planning. Mitigation is about problem avoidance, while contingency is more about problem recovery. Clearly, there can be overlaps between the two ideas. For example, in the case of fire risk, mitigation is about banning smoking, checking wiring, or not allowing barbecues in dry woodlands. Contingency, on the other hand, is about having fire extinguishers, evacuation procedures, first aid training, etc.

Making this distinction raises interesting questions about how we approach risk in strategy. Mitigating risk, in my view, is part of the strategy development process. In some cases, it may be right to mitigate risk; in other cases not. Often there are costs or consequences involved in mitigation. I will talk more about this in a later section on risk-return and 'Make or Buy' decisions.

Contingency planning, on the other hand, may be about diluting the strategy – not really committing to the strategic decision. If I have a costly recovery plan, what does this say about my belief in my strategy? In 1519, Hernan Cortez destroyed his ships on the coast of Mexico to eliminate the option of retreat, prior to conquering Mexico with only 600 men. This mimicked a similar tactic employed by Alexander the

Great prior to conquering Persia: burning the ships to prevent the option of retreat clarifies the importance and belief in the advancement plan. On the other hand, they undoubtedly should have put more life-boats on the *Titanic*. The only other logical option would have been to have none at all, so everyone bought in to the 'unsinkable' mindset.

A most interesting area where this distinction is debated relates to safety systems in cars, which a client of mine specialized in producing. There have been safety systems in cars for some time in the form of seat belts, and more recently air bags, to soften impact in the case of an accident. These are now called 'passive safety systems', to differentiate them from the 'active safety systems' that this client has recently started to develop. This is electronic equipment that uses a combination of sensors and computers to calculate the likelihood of an accident at any point of time, and apply braking a lot faster than a human to avoid the accident altogether. The argument is that if your active safety system (your risk mitigation mechanism) is 100 per cent effective, you don't need a passive safety system (your contingency mechanism). But the question is who will be the first manufacturer to put their head above the parapet and offer a car with an active but no passive safety system?

Generic forms of mitigation

I believe that there are two main types of mitigation: one is about information and analysis, and the other is about sharing. I'll cover both in some depth. But before I do, first let me explain where I get my view that there are two types.

Let me refer you back to my Character Profiling model, which has three dimensions: Bold Creative, Empathic and Self-Disciplined. My hypothesis is that these three dimensions are MECE – an acronym which spelt out stands for Mutually Exclusive and Collectively Exhaustive. This is a term that I believe was invented by the consultancy firm McKinsey and is used primarily for developing options as a solution to a clearly defined problem. For example, if the problem is that you arrive at a crossroads and you don't know which way to go, the MECE options would be turn left, turn right or straight across. They are exclusive (ME) because you cannot move in a combination of these options. And they are exhaustive (CE) because there are no other options available. So my hypothesis is that these three dimensions of character cover all aspects of character, but that they do not influence each other in any way. Another way of describing this hypothesis, for those with a mathematical bent, is that they are orthogonal.

This means that, in the context of risk, and if you are a risk taker, then your character is naturally Bold Creative. We can dilute the impact of this character attribute, without actually reducing it, by also having character strength that moves towards one of the other dimensions, namely Empathic or Self-Disciplined. Moving towards the Empathic dimension is relating to others, which is a process that shares some of the personal risk that you would have taken, had you acted on your own. Moving towards the Self-Disciplined dimension is about seeking information, either to support an otherwise risky decision, or to be able to take early action before a danger fully materializes. This is moving away from an intuitive response to risk, to a more analytical response. Or to use my favourite metaphors, moving from tiger to elephant.

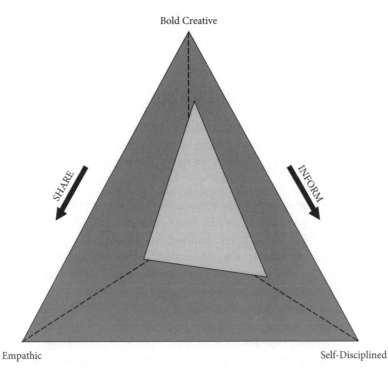

Figure 5.1 Generic approaches to mitigation

We can think of two generic mitigation strategies in a number of ways. For example, early mankind responded to the danger of being attacked by forming into tribes. Apart from the fact that this made them stronger as a group, the added advantage was that they shared the risk of being harmed. I am reminded of the joke about the two explorers being pursued by an angry bear. One puts on his running shoes, and the other says to him: 'Don't be foolish. You can't outrun a bear!' The one with the running shoes then says: 'I don't need to outrun the bear, I just need to outrun you!'

Once a tribe is formed, then lookouts are posted in the trees and on higher ground. What is that about? An early warning system is a way of providing information about the likelihood of a dangerous situation, so that action can be taken.

In classic risk management processes, we think of mitigation in terms of controls, which are typically a combination of sharing and inform-ing. They are sharing because they involve others in the process. They are informing because the controls are normally based on measuring certain factors which are indicators of the likelihood of a dangerous situation being realized. So for example, a bank lending money to a client company will manage the risk of default by asking the company to provide regular financial reports. Certain indicators such as profit margin, net current assets and cash flow projections help inform the likelihood of a company running into difficulties and not being able to repay the loan. In encouraging these kinds of reporting disciplines, the bank is also effectively sharing more of the risk with the client company.

At a personal leadership level, we use what we call the Stacey Matrix (See Figure 5.2), which is an adaptation of a model proposed by Ralph Stacey (Shaw & Stacey, 2006), a professor in management at the University of Hertfordshire, as a way of thinking about when to share risk associated with certain decisions. Stacey's work was triggered by an examination of Chaos Theory (sometimes referred to as the Butterfly Effect), which essentially is that even though systems have linked cause and effect, and therefore outcomes are perfectly predictable, chaotic systems are those where very small changes in causes can have hugely different effects or outcomes. So applying this to organizational leader-ship situations, it means that getting certain key decisions slightly wrong can have a disproportionately big impact on the organization.

The Stacey Matrix is a simple but powerful model for thinking about approaches to leadership decision making. Situations where there are high levels of 'certainty' and agreement are good homes for structure and control – the implication is that individuals can make good decisions and are indeed responsible for doing so. However, where there is high uncertainty and disagreement, that is, what I would define as higher risk situations, possibly even chaotic, the Stacey Matrix suggests a different approach which has two components: experimentation, which is about getting more information before making the bigger decisions; and collaboration, sharing the process of decision making, and thus sharing the risk.

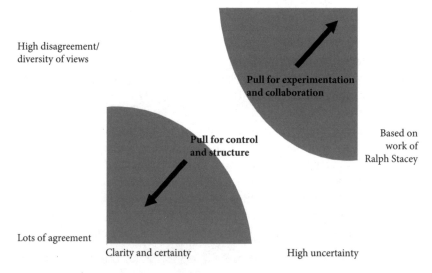

Figure 5.2 Adapting management styles

As a commercial director in our consultancy business unit at Ashridge Business School, I found this a very helpful model for dealing with risk in decision making. I was holding responsibility for day-to-day commercial, financial and legal decisions on a large number of client projects, involving a number of professional consultants and support staff. I was part of a leadership team, with whom I had meetings approximately monthly and had more regular exchange or email. The rest of the team all had other roles, in many cases doing work directly with clients on projects – I was the one holding these kinds of decisions on a daily basis. Deferring every decision to the rest of the team would have paralysed the business, so I had to decide which ones to take and which ones to consult. Put another way, for which decisions do I take the risk personally, because if I get it wrong, there are likely to be personal repercussions, and for which decisions do I share the risk, by consulting with the rest of the team. Stacey's model was a valuable way of thinking about when to consult, or when to collaborate.

At other times, the decision-making process is more about getting additional information prior to making the decision. Pricing of new contracts was a case in point, as our pricing model was deliberately variable. I was regularly asked: 'what daily fee rate can I pitch this piece of work in at?' In those instances where colleagues were advising me that the client would not pay our standard or target rate, there was a decision to be made which involved risk. The risk if we didn't reduce the rate was that we wouldn't win a significant piece of new business. The risk if we did reduce the rate was that our profit margin would be adversely affected and, more to the point, we would set a precedent that we would accept a lower price on other projects.

To reduce the risk, one of the important pieces of information was the level of overall utilization of our salaried consultants. At one stage, the utilization rate was particularly low, so I supported the decision to price low to win important new business for these consultants. The improvement in overall profitability more than justified the risk of setting an unhealthy precedent. At a later stage, when a similar pricing question was posed, our utilization was much higher. We didn't respond on price, and effectively walked away from the business opportunity. In this instance, the information about utilization satisfied me that the risk of margin dilution and setting the wrong precedent were no longer worth taking.

These tended to be more tactical decisions. At a more strategic level, the 'share' mitigation model comes to play in 'Make or Buy' decisions and a whole approach to partnership. An example of 'inform' mitigation can be seen in how we approach innovation, and what do we need to know before we press the button on a major new investment. For example, Procter & Gamble (P&G) is one of the better examples of effective innovation through major successful global product launches or re-launches. In this sense, they appear to be specialists in taking strategic risks. But they manage the risk of innovation through extensive testing before committing to a launch. One of the planks of P&G's global strategy, as set out by Lafley and Martin (2013), is a core competence in what they call 'Go to market'. And one of the cornerstones of this capability is their effectiveness in researching and testing prior to major launch, to be confident that the risks of failure are substantially reduced at the time of the launch.

But extensive testing before launching carries costs – both in monetary terms and, crucially, in time. And in the long run, time costs money. Delaying a launch of a new product will often lead to lower lifetime profitability for that product, as competitors either get there first or catch up more quickly.

The 'share' mitigation option is generally the 'Buy' as opposed to 'Make'. And while this may be lower risk, it generally comes with higher costs.

There is a trade-off for reduced risk. Financial analysts have extensive models for understanding this trade-off. Business leaders are generally aware of these trade-offs more extensively. We are talking financial risk and specifically 'risk-return' thinking.

Risk-return

Risk-return thinking says that there is an implicit reward for taking risk. It's not guaranteed, of course, such is the nature of risk. But in the long run, or on balance, the thinking is that if you take more risk, you can expect a better reward.

This is played out, and indeed measured, in financial trading markets, where returns are the financial amounts that investors can receive back on their investments. In the case of stock market investments, these returns correlate closely to the profits made by companies, which are published on a regular, generally quarterly, basis.

The risk in financial markets is measured as variability over time or between investments, as I touched on in Chapter 4 when talking about definition of risk. This may be variability of share price, or indeed profit, or some other important measure. So an investment where this key measure varies a lot over time is higher risk than one where the measure is more stable. This risk and variability tend to follow patterns by certain groupings of investments, for example, by industry sector. So a new technology sector such as biotechnology, with smaller companies and unproven technology, would be a higher risk sector than consumer goods, which has established large organizations with mostly established brands and technologies. According to our risk-return thinking, we would expect to get a higher return from an investment in the biomedical sector compared to the consumer goods sector.

As we explored in Chapter 4, one way in which we represent this variability is through the normal curve, sometimes called the bell curve. For example, our likely financial returns in a given sector are distributed around our expected return, the peak of the normal curve. If there is a wide range of expected returns, this is a high-risk situation which is represented by the wide normal curve. A lower risk sector with a smaller range of possible returns is represented by the taller, narrower normal curve.

If we build our risk-return thinking into our normal curve model, and combine our broad, high-risk curve with our narrow low-risk curve, we end up with something that looks like the diagram below (Figure 5.3). First of all, in the low-risk case, represented by the taller, narrower curve, our expected outcome or return is more likely than in our high-risk case; hence it is taller. Moreover, the expected return or outcome from our high-risk option is higher than the expected return from our lower-risk option. This is risk-return thinking. And the difference in return between the two options is referred to as the risk premium.

Let's look at this diagram in more detail, as it highlights a fascinating insight when we look at risk in this way. There are two shaded areas in the diagram. The shaded area on the left, what I have called the area of danger, is the main reason why we may not go for the higher risk option. This represents all those possible outcomes or returns that are worse than our expected outcome, and which are more likely to occur if we choose the high-risk option.

But now look at the shaded area on the right side. This is the area of opportunity, and represents all the outcomes or returns that are better

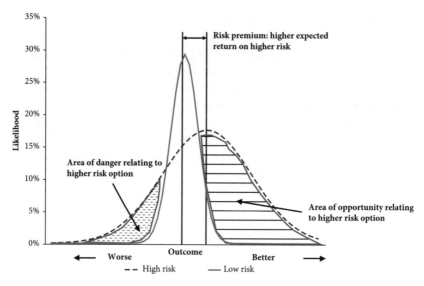

Figure 5.3 Risk premium in statistical variability

than our expected outcome, which are more likely to occur if we select the high-risk option. What is interesting is that this is a much bigger area than our area of danger. This is because, when we look at risk in this way, there are two important assumptions that lead us to this place.

1. Our risk profile is symmetrical as represented by a normal curve. That means that better than expected outcomes are just as likely to occur as worse than expected outcomes. This is clearly not the way we always think about risk, and when we think of it in terms of possible crisis situations, it generally doesn't have this symmetry. But in the case of financial investment, and more generally, business innovation, it probably often does.
2. Risk-return thinking is valid. We should expect on average to earn more from a high-risk investment than a low-risk one.

When looked at like this, there is quite a compelling case for taking more risk. Our chances of doing better are disproportionately higher than our chances of doing worse.

It begs the question, if we saw business investment in this way more clearly, would we be inclined to take more risk?

The reality appears to be that we tend to be drawn to focus more on the smaller shaded danger zone on the left, almost like Greek sailors to the siren call. This leads to the phenomenon of 'loss aversion', which I shall pick up in more detail in Chapter 7 when I talk about illusions and traps.

Risk-return in strategic decision making – 'Make' or 'Buy'

If we think about expected outcomes in terms of projected profit to a business, then one of the key strategic decisions we can make to impact variability of profit is the 'Make' or 'Buy' decision.

This means that for a particular process, and for a range of products or services, business leaders are faced with a trade-off. They need to decide whether to operate or make in-house, inside the business, or whether to buy in product or services from another business organization. Apart from an assessment of capability, which is clearly critical in these decisions, a key factor is the flexibility of the costs associated. To simplify the model for illustration, costs associated with the 'Make' option tend to be largely fixed. This means they don't tend to change with short-term changes in our sales income. Costs associated with the 'Buy' options tend to be more variable. They do tend to change as our sales income changes.

When we think about risk as variability, the underlying variable is our level of sales. In other words, we encounter risk if and when we cannot predict our sales that accurately. However, while that is the source of variability, the real risk is in what happens to the financial outcome that we care most about as managers – our profit. As most businesses will testify, profit is generally much more variable than sales. And this is made all the worse the higher proportion of costs that are fixed.

This was brought home to me most vividly when I worked as a consultant for one of the major leisure travel firms in the UK. The business model for my client, as for the whole industry, was about acquiring a large number of strategic assets, specifically planes, boats and hotels, and trying to fill them at an optimal price. For many years, the economics worked well in terms of being able to offer low prices on holidays by getting high utilization on these assets.

However, these were financially high-risk businesses, because a high proportion of the costs were fixed. They had to pay almost the same amount to finance, maintain and fuel a plane that was full of passengers as they had to, a plane that was half-empty – but the income for the half-empty plane would potentially be half as much. In a buoyant market, over the course of an average season, the combined income on full planes and not-so-full planes was enough to cover the fixed costs and make a respectable profit.

Then the 9/11 terrorist attacks happened, and the plane-based travel markets stalled. It was no longer buoyant. And the high fixed-cost model suddenly became a huge liability. My client had to be rescued, with a consortium of bankers hovering around anxiously as the rescue operation unfolded. A key element of the rescue plan was to reduce the fixed to variable cost ratio considerably.

This might seem obvious but wasn't as straightforward as you can imagine, due to the mindset of the management team that had presided over the company during the hazy days of success. An illustration of this was a snippet of a conversation with one of the senior managers. 'We believed that we were making £X mn profit with Y planes on the books. So the way to improve our situation was to double the number of planes; so that we can double the profit.'

A good way to understand this kind of strategic financial risk is to look at a Finance 101 tool, the break-even chart.

Break-even and financial gearing

Our break-even charts (Figure 5.4) show two different business models from a financial perspective: a high gearing model that represents high financial risk and a low gearing model that shows low financial risk.

To recap on the break-even chart for those who can't remember Finance 101 or never encountered it, on the chart we plot the level of units sales output on the horizontal x-axis, and money on the vertical y-axis. The chart is designed to predict our profit at different levels of unit sales output. We do this by plotting three lines. The first one, the solid one, is our revenue line. This is the relationship between the level of unit sales output and the money we receive. As it assumes we have a fixed unit price, it is a straight line – money is directly proportional to unit sales. So if we double our unit sales, we double the amount of money we receive.

The next line to look at is the horizontal dotted line. This is our fixed cost line. This represents the amount of money we have to pay for fixed costs at different levels of unit sales output. In contrast to our revenue line, this, as the name suggests, does not vary with unit sales output. However much sales output we achieve, we still pay the same amount in fixed costs.

Then we have the angled dotted 'variable + fixed cost line'. This plots the total amount of money we need to pay out in cost at different levels of unit sales output. As implied by the name, it is made up of two parts. The fixed cost, hence it is superimposed above the fixed cost line in terms of money – y-axis. The variable cost part, like the revenue line, varied in proportion to the level of unit sales output. It is not as steep as the revenue line because hopefully our variable cost per unit of sales is lower than our revenue per unit of sales – that is, our price. So again as unit sales output doubles, our variable cost also doubles. But unlike the revenue line, the 'variable + fixed cost line' starts at the level of fixed costs and increases from there.

So how does this help us determine profit? That is represented by the gap, in money terms, between our revenue line and the total cost line (i.e. the variable + fixed cost line). At zero unit sales output, we make a thumping loss equivalent to the full impact of our fixed costs: that is, the gap between the revenue line, which is at zero, and the cost line, which is at the level of our total costs.

As the level of unit sales output increases, we move to the right of the chart, and the gap reduces. Our loss reduces until we reach a point where the revenue line and the total cost (variable + fixed cost) lines intersect. And that is what is known as the break-even point. It is the point in terms of unit sales output where our revenue and total costs are the same. We break even. And as we go beyond this point, to the right on the chart, we start to make a profit, as measured by the gap between the revenue line and the total cost line.

Having explained what the chart means, what is the difference between the high gearing and the low gearing models? What are these charts saying to us? Simply that the high gearing model has a higher proportion of fixed costs in the total cost mix – it's more akin to the travel model mentioned earlier. Even at the break-even point, represented by the solid vertical line, the fixed costs are still the lion's share of the costs, compared to the variable costs. In the low gearing model on the right, the opposite is the case: the fixed costs are a small proportion of the total costs, at the break-even point.

So why does this have an impact on financial risk? The answer is in looking what happens to the profit in the two models – the profit being the gap between the revenue line and the total cost line. At the break-even point, it is about the same. No difference there then. The point is what happens to profit as the unit sales output varies around the break-even point. For the same variation around this point, as marked by the dotted vertical lines, the profit in the low gearing model decreases and increases slightly – actually slightly more in percentage terms than the changes in unit sales.

However, in the high gearing model, as the unit sales output increases above break-even, there is a disproportionately high increase in profit – it more than doubles. However, as the unit sales output decreases, we quickly move into a loss-making situation. This is in a nutshell how gearing impacts financial risk.

As commercial director at Ashridge, this aspect of gearing was an important part of the strategic discussions that we had. The consulting business had a large number of non-salaried associate consultants working with us. During my time in the role, we were able to significantly improve the profitability of the business, without seeing a large increase in sales revenue. The biggest single factor was in making more of the variability of our cost base as a result of having a pool of variable cost resource, our associates, and transferring more work to our fixed-cost base, our salaried consultants. In doing this, some of my colleagues on the board wanted to take steps to remove associates altogether from our resources. I argued strongly against doing this, as having a mix of salaried and

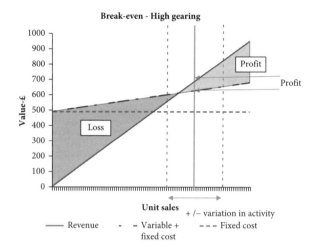

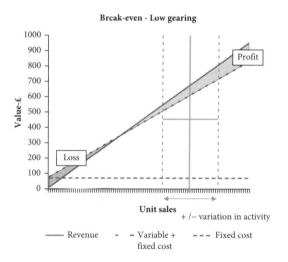

Figure 5.4 Managing risk through gearing

associate consultants is a key factor in our ability to manage financial risk more effectively. A model that was exclusively based on salaried consultants, in a market where predicting sales output is very challenging, would in my view have given us too heavy a burden of financial risk.

Consequently, the natural question would be: if it reduces risk, why not only work with associate non-salaried consultants? In the travel company scenario, why own anything? Why not buy or lease assets as they are needed – this would considerably de-risk the situation?

For the financial answer to this question, we refer again to our risk-return thinking. Reduced risk comes at a cost. One of the more difficult conversations with some management colleagues at Ashridge was, why were we paying our associates at a higher rate per day than we were paying our internal salaried consultants and faculty?

The answer is clearly because we have transferred the risk, the financial risk that comes from variability of sales outcomes, to them. Risk taking deserves a reward; reducing risk costs money.

Not understanding this is probably the biggest factor of which I am aware that can lead to business failure.

Ansoff Roulette

Risk-return is fundamental to how gambling works. The more risk in the potential outcome, the more you stand to gain. One of the most visual displays of quantifiable risk is the roulette table. If you place your bets in one of the big boxes, the red or the black, the odds or the evens, the risk otherwise expressed as the odds are low. There is almost a 50 per cent chance that you will win. The return reflects this – you can only double your bet in winnings. If you place your bet on a smaller single number square, your risk is much higher. You have slightly less than 1 in 36 chance of winning. But if you win, you get 36 times your bet.

At the same time, one of the more visual ways of thinking about business strategic decisions, under competitive conditions, is the Ansoff matrix.

Igor Ansoff in his book *Corporate Strategy*, written in the 1960s, proposed a diagram as a way of systematically considering strategic growth options, which consisted of a box with four quadrants. Was this the original 'matrix', as subsequently used in other box diagrams produced by strategic consultancies like the Boston Consulting Group?

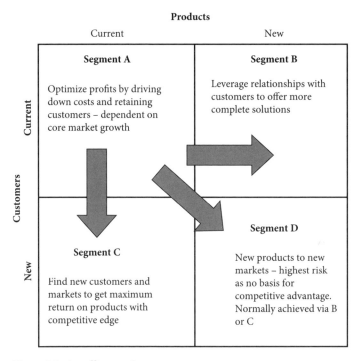

Products

Current   New

	Current	New
Segment A	Optimize profits by driving down costs and retaining customers – dependent on core market growth	**Segment B** Leverage relationships with customers to offer more complete solutions
Segment C	Find new customers and markets to get maximum return on products with competitive edge	**Segment D** New products to new markets – highest risk as no basis for competitive advantage. Normally achieved via B or C

Figure 5.5 Ansoff's mattrix

Ansoff proposed that two key growth dimensions that should be considered were 'products' and 'markets', and each dimension was split into 'current' and 'new'. The idea is that organizations consider where growth opportunities existed, with current products they already produce, in current markets where they already operate; or alternatively, new products in current markets, or current products in new products, etc. Clearly, the growth opportunities from venturing into new products and/or new markets must be significantly greater than from sticking in the current zones, so if growth were the only consideration, you would place all your bets in the new boxes.

However, there is a catch – increased risk. Why increased risk? There is a sense that when we work with products we already know well, or in markets we already know, or more to the point, where we are already known, we are less likely to lose out financially than if we are moving into unfamiliar areas of knowledge. And this appears to be generally borne out by experience.

However, we must ask what is the real nature of the risk of going new instead of current. The essence of it is that we know less – we have less information about the new and what happens when we operate in that area. We can estimate how we think we will do in the new – forecast expected sales or profit – but the likelihood of our being right is much lower. The degree of variability of possible outcomes is much higher – in this sense, the risk is higher. But so too is the potential reward.

When I used Ansoff as a framework in a strategic workshop with a client, we called the process Ansoff Roulette. We spent a lot of the work-shop reviewing different projects which offered growth opportunities. We then drew up an Ansoff Roulette table and decided where we would place each of the projects on the table. To what extent were we looking at launching new products, and in some cases straying into new prod-uct technology? To what extent were we proposing to operate in new markets – either new geographical markets, or new sectors, or even new channels or decision makers within existing sectors? Then each member of the team had a certain number of chips, representing their votes on how to invest the limited growth funds available. We ended up with a set of strategic options with which everyone felt comfortable.

There was an interesting point in the meeting when I pointed out to the team that the further their project strayed from the top-left quadrant – the current product/current market quadrant – the more risk they were taking on.

There were heated protests from those who had proposed the more adventurous projects. That was until I pointed out that, just like a roulette table, while the odds of winnings may be longer, the potential winnings were also higher to compensate. This led to a new level of enthusiasm in approaching the exercise, and some robust and useful discussion.

We see in this situation a good example of how perception of what we mean by 'risk' can have a significant influence on the process for making strategic decisions. If we see 'risk' primarily as increased danger and a higher likelihood of experiencing harm, we are less inclined to vote for

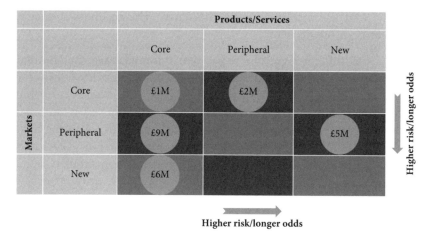

Figure 5.6 Ansoff roulette

a strategic option which carries more risk. If we see 'risk' as increased variability of possible outcome, with as much upside as downside potential around our estimated outcome, then we become more likely to vote for the riskier option. If at the same time, we add that the expected outcome from the riskier option is better than the expected outcome from the less risky option, we are even more likely again to place our bets on the 'new-new' strategic options.

This Ansoff Roulette model worked well for this client, who has since had a high degree of success in implementing the strategy.

The dangers of misunderstanding risk-return

One of the best examples of how the risk-return mechanism substantially impacts business models is in the clothing retail sector. There are two distinct extremes of clothing retailing, and I have consulted extensively in both. These are discount clothing and fashion clothing. The biggest difference between the two is clearly price – the price that can be charged for the same amount of textile material of a similar quality. And the second biggest difference? The business model is completely different.

Discount clothing is high volume per item, minimal variety and limited write-offs. Fashion retailing is low volume per item, high level of variety and generally high levels of write-offs. These two models carry big differences in terms of risk. In discount clothing, the risk is minimal because a high proportion of stock gets sold eventually. And the high volume is more likely to cover the biggest costs in retail – staff and space – so margins can be small. The risk in fashion retail is high. Because it has to innovate constantly, there is a high write-off cost – there is risk that some lines may not sell at all. The volumes are lower, so the margins have to be high to be able to cover costs.

As a result, not understanding this, or attempting to move between models, can be hazardous. I worked for a novelty retailer (not in clothing) that was failing to generate enough profit margin to cover financing costs. They attributed the problem to high write-off of stock. My view was that this was the risk associated with their business model. In reality, their pricing policy, which led to relatively low margins, failed to recognize the risk in their business model. With their innovative proposition, sales were not that sensitive to increases in prices at the margin. They could price higher without losing much in sales, and increase the gross margin. And due to the risk in the business, and the cost associated with that risk manifesting mainly in stock write-offs, they needed to.

An understanding of risk was about understanding the key variables in the business, understanding how they interacted with each other. It is this understanding that is critical to good strategy making.

But this understanding is not always formal, not always purely analytical, and not always able to be worked out with the luxury of a stretch of time. Sometimes, it is informal, intuitive and fast. Sometimes it is tiger territory.

The impact of risk on the value of capital

Financial investors and analysts take a view on the value of potential investments (i.e. capital) by projecting/forecasting expected returns on a year-by-year basis, and combining these with an assessment of the risk of the investment, as determined by the variability of expected returns. There is a well-defined and accepted calculation for doing this, known as the net present value (NPV). Essentially, the investment is valued by adding up all the future cash returns (i.e. the cash surplus after deducting cash expenses from cash income, by year). Then the value of each future cash return is discounted for every year it is projected to occur in the future, by a percentage known as the annual discount factor. This factor is made up of two parts added together. The first part is the percentage cost of money – this is that part of the interest rate that you would have to pay to borrow money where there is no risk of it not being repaid. This is largely the case with highly secured lending as in mortgages, where any inability to repay is covered by selling the property to repay. The second part is the risk factor. This is a more subjective factor based on how risky the investment is – that is, how much variability there is in expected returns. So the bigger the range of possible returns, the bigger the risk, the bigger the risk factor and the more the projected cash return is discounted. When you add up all the fully discounted future cash returns by year, you end up with the NPV, which represents a view of the value of the investment.

This works relatively well with investments relating to businesses that are already generating positive cash returns, but slightly less well with those that are generating cash income but not necessarily surpluses. The issue arises with new ventures that have no track record of generating cash income, which is the case for many innovation projects. The question is how to value an innovation project. Even if you have a view of risk, you have a limited view of return.

This is the zone where elephants struggle. This, I suggest, is the domain of tigers.

When a venture like Google or Twitter is brought to the market, how do investors value the investment? There is often no clear view of how cash will be generated, never mind how much of it. And yet investors do indeed value it. As a group, they will talk each other into a valuation, which is based largely on intuition. There may be guesses as to how much cash may be generated at various points in the future, but a guess is all they can be. It's all about gut and passion, and quick thinking in the heat of the financial market. It's tiger territory. And as we have seen, tigers are quite different from elephants.

Chapter 6

Tigers and informal risk

Steve Jobs has been quoted as saying: 'Don't let the noise of others' opinions drown out your inner voice. Have the courage to follow your heart and intuition'.

Bill Treasurer in his book *Right Risk* (2003) says that 'The greatest reward for each Right Risk taker is an intimate encounter with the magnificence of your own soul'.

When we came across tigers in our research into how leaders work with risk, the participant who introduced us to the metaphor described them as intuitive, fast and colourful, but you don't need too many or it can become chaotic. There is something dangerous about connecting with your intuition, but somehow this strikes to the heart of our humanity. It cannot be ignored as it's part of what makes us who we are, but we need to watch out that it doesn't get overplayed, set loose without constraint, because the tiger in us is truly wild.

The tiger in us struggles with the idea that you need to minimize risk. Why? Because it represents the land of opportunity much more so than the land of danger and harm. And the problem is that as soon as you stop to analyse or calculate, you are already engaged in minimizing risk, whether you like it or not.

Tigers are intuitive instead of calculating. There tends to be more emotion involved in the decision-making process. Passion has a role to play. There is a belief that the best way to learn about risk is not to study it or analyse it but to take it.

Some colleagues at Ashridge recently ran an expo trip to Silicon Valley, for a client group from the Middle East. The aim was to learn something about how Silicon Valley championed innovation. They visited companies like Google, Apple, Tesla, Intel, Facebook, HP and Singularity University. One thing they discovered was that risk taking is a basic part of the culture, and failure is the seal of approval. It's almost a rite of initiation into the community. If you haven't failed, you haven't tried hard enough. The skill is not in avoiding failure, but in failing fast and learning fast.

Elephants are 'Be perfect'; tigers are 'Hurry up'

Perfection is not as highly valued by tigers as it is by elephants. As an executive coach, this is probably the single biggest issue that my clients wrestle with as they take on more senior roles and strive to become better leaders. Often, they have achieved higher levels of responsibility by being technically good at what they do. They have experienced working in well-defined processes where attention to detail is important – where being right more often than wrong has been part of the basis of recognition. They have built on the experience of their education, where getting the most right answers or putting together the most rationally persuasive arguments has been the basis for the best grades.

One of the things we look at as coaches is the underlying motivation that drives the behaviour of the people we are coaching. The point is that these are often sources of stress, and can therefore undermine the resilience of leaders. While they may have contributed to career success up to a point, they can become factors that derail leaders under pressure. There appear to be three favourite drivers – favourite in the sense of being most highly evident in my coaching experience from Kahler's original list of five (1975): 'Be perfect', 'Please others' and 'Hurry up'.

For prospective leaders who are likely to experience increased levels of uncertainty in making decisions, letting go of their 'Be perfect' drivers is often one of the biggest challenges. Their identity and the way they evaluate their career progression is often around 'being right' or having a well-reasoned or evidenced argument. Some organizations have a culture that encourages this to high levels of management. Procter & Gamble (P&G) overtly rewards 'Be perfect' behaviour through career progression as it is part of their culture – being confident of the evidence before taking bigger decisions. I talk about this in more depth in the later section on 'Faith' in Chapter 13 while considering what leaders put their faith in, when working with risk.

I find that in the coaching 'room' – I use room figuratively because often these conversations are conducted over the phone – there are better ways of framing the idea of letting go of the 'Be perfect' driver. I challenge the coachee to consider how to work effectively with risk, rather than avoid it; that this is something of the essence of leadership. The challenge is about making more room for intuition, in the place of rational analysis. And what is interesting is that we model this behaviour as coaches – we make room for intuition. Some refer to this as part of a Gestalt approach, or staying in the present. This links to the growing body of work on mindfulness, which several of my Ashridge colleagues are promoting. The intuition that develops from a more 'mindful' approach to coaching situations can often be the key to making real progress with an issue with which the coachee may be struggling. When we are learning to be more effective coaches, we may start with looking at how we listen more actively to the content of what is being said. We will then try focussing on trying to observe the emotional aspects of what the coachee is saying, through voice timbre and body language. Last but not the least, we will pay attention to what our intuition or our gut is telling us, sometimes to develop a hypothesis about 'what is not being said'. By nature, this feels risky because we can be wrong – but somehow even if we are apparently wrong (which may be deduced based on the coachee's response), the process excites a different dynamic in the conversation, which moves it to a different level. While the elephant-side is looking at the safer analysis and understanding of the content, the tiger-side is engaging with the more risky gut feeling.

And we may mirror this thinking in how we encourage our client, the coachee, to address 'Be Perfect'. One tip is to deliberately try something that you know has a high chance of being wrong, but where the consequences of error are small: to start to acclimatize to the uncomfortable feeling of maybe being shown to be wrong. This is often a big leap into the unknown for our prospective leaders. Not only does it go against our social conditioning, but there's often a persistently nagging inner voice that is saying: 'don't be a fool!'. What is intriguing about our natural resilience is that when we do jump, but it proves to be wrong and we end up with egg on our face, there is something of the other voice inside us that regardless says: 'Let's try that one again!' This is the tiger in us, asking the elephant to step aside.

This appears to be something of the spirit of Silicon Valley, specialists in the art of letting go of 'Be perfect'. You win your spurs by failing fast, not because you have some masochistic tendency to be hurt, but because of this reflex action that calls out to you to 'get up, dust yourself off and try again'.

What's interesting when we talk to tigers about drivers is that they do appear to have a driver – the 'Hurry up' driver. Tigers move quickly, because they move intuitively; they are not waiting for more evidence to support their case. So they are particularly useful where speed is critical. In technology, this is more the case than in, say, grocery consumer goods or construction. The issue in technology is that if you are not fast enough, someone else will get there before you – and often, but not always, being first mover leads to important competitive advantage. This has proven to be largely the case in Silicon Valley – the first icon-based computer interface, the first search engine based on sophisticated literature referencing knowledge, the first social media site based on personal graphics, etc. Tigers seem to try, fail, try, fail, try, fail, try and succeed, but once they do succeed, they appear to emerge ahead of other animals.

Speed is often important in combat. Military strategy is primarily focused on beating the enemy. We explore this in more depth in Chapter 8 when I look at cases of victory in conflict situations, but suffice to say that one of the proven effective ways to beat the opposition is to pre-empt them. Being faster to act not only increases the chances of seizing important strategic assets, but also creates increased uncertainty, and thence fear, on the part of the enemy. And this can be the key to success.

So tigers have an important role to play in military leadership. Intuition is a key factor. Tigers are naturally courageous, and prepared to take risk with inadequate information – they are greater risks because of inadequate information. Does this mean that we only want tigers in military leadership, and that elephants have no role to play? Absolutely not – and I will explore this issue in more depth in Chapter 8.

Tigers, elephants, the drivers and the character profiler

Here, I want to draw a few strands of thinking together.

I talked about the three most common of Kahler's drivers: 'Be perfect', 'Please others' and 'Hurry up'. And I have suggested that our tigers are more likely to have a 'Hurry up' driver, and our elephants are more likely to have a 'Be perfect' driver. So what of the 'Please others' driver? Is this not picked up by either animal, and irrelevant for either mode of working with risk?

Then I thought of the Blonay Character Profiler, and realized that there is some connection between these drivers and the character attributes. 'Be perfect' seems to sit more closely with 'Self-Disciplined'. 'Hurry up', by virtue of this being seen more as a tiger trait, connects more closely with 'Bold Creative'. So we have our third driver, 'Please others' which clearly could find a home more closely aligned with the 'Empathic' attribute.

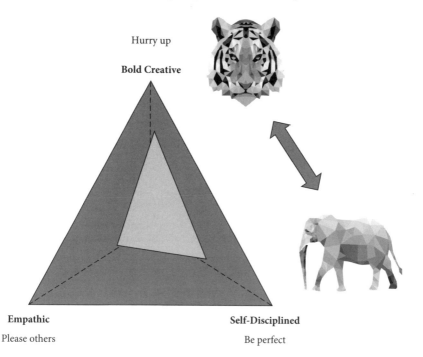

Figure 6.1 Personality drivers for tigers and elephants

So we have a dynamic expressed as Bold Creative tigers, with 'Hurry up' drivers in tension with Self-Disciplined Be perfect elephants. Meanwhile, the Empathic 'Please others' look on from the sidelines and don't have much to contribute to the issue of how to work with risk.

But then I note that we have already expressed the idea that elephants have two ways of mitigating risk. One is the 'Inform' route, which leads us towards the Self-Disciplined end of the spectrum, and the other is the 'Share' route, which leads us towards the Empathic end – for example, the Stacey idea that we can deal with uncertainty by collaborating, that is, sharing ideas. In this sense, I believe our elephants occupy both of the lower two attributes in our profiler. Elephants are by nature social animals – it's all about the fellowship of the herd!

Meanwhile, our tiger stands resolutely isolated as the Bold Creative, with a 'Hurry up' driver.

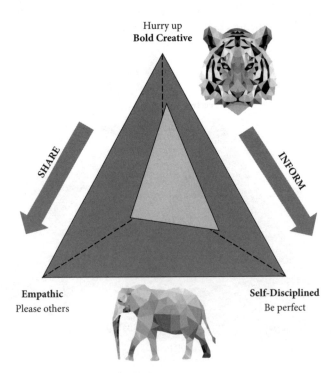

Figure 6.2 Tigers as risk takers; elephants as mitigators

Tigers and information

Tigers are highly selective about their use of information. They tend to scan it rather than analyse it. They have a natural inclination to look for shortcuts and signals. They have phobia against paralysis by analysis.

Malcolm Gladwell in his book *Blink* (2006) tells stories of how information can get in the way of intuitive decision making where there are risks involved. He talks about the fact that in the Second World War, the Americans were taken completely by surprise by the Japanese invasion of Pearl Harbour, but it wasn't because they didn't know enough about Japanese intentions. They had broken codes and were reading Japanese mail. He argues that they were overwhelmed with information. Ironically, journalists who knew a lot less were predicting a Japanese attack. He says the key to good decision making is not knowledge, but understanding.

Gladwell also tells the story how too much information has got in the way of effective health diagnosis and decision making. Brendan Reilly was chairman of the Department of Medicine at Cook County Hospital in Chicago in the late 1990s. The Emergency Department, which had 250,000 patients per year, had a problem with how to direct resources to those who needed it most. This was particularly the case for effective diagnosis of chest pains as potential heart attacks. The issue was that when a patient came in with chest pain, there was an extensive process of information gathering using interviews and measuring equipment. In spite of this, the resulting estimates of likely heart attack were not very accurate. The problem was that most doctors corrected for their uncertainty by erring heavily on the side of caution. 'As long as there is a chance that someone might be having a heart attack, why take even the smallest risk by ignoring the problem?' But bed capacity was a growing issue. So Reilly commissioned a cardiologist named Lee Goldman, who analysed hundreds of cases to look at what factors best predicted heart attack. He came up with an algorithm – an equation – which could be represented as a simple decision tree, taking a lot of the guesswork out of treating chest pains. It was based on relatively few key factors, and no one wanted to believe it was right. They didn't believe that a simple equation could perform better than a trained physician. Reilly persevered, and agreed to run his algorithm alongside the opinions of the physicians for two years. Goldman's algorithm won easily: 70 per cent better at predicting those who were not having a heart attack, and 16 per cent better at predicting those who were (95 per cent versus 82 per cent). The conclusion: 'extra information isn't actually an advantage, in fact it's more than useless, it's harmful'. The problem is that 'doctors think it's mundane to follow guidelines, it's much more gratifying to come up with a decision on your own ... algorithm's don't feel right' (Gladwell, 2006).

I am currently working with a financial services client that specializes in property investment. They are one of the leading players in the global property market, and they have a conundrum. They have been generally quite successful in making smart investments because they have developed processes for measuring risk and then asking clients to make clearly defined trade-offs between risk and return. Measuring risk is the clever bit – as is typical in financial services, they define risk as variability, and actually seek to calculate the standard deviation of historic returns for similar investments. In other words, they use the normal bell curve as a picture of risk. They break this down into country variability, variability due to leverage between debt and equity, variability due to the stage in the property lifecycle, the status of the property (built, leased, etc.) and the type of contract. And a summary of all this information gets presented to an approval committee.

What is the issue? All of this takes time. And like most businesses, they have an aspiration to grow. To do that, they need to build the confidence of their clients in them. To do that, they need to outperform the competition, get a better return. Part of that is being able to assess risk accurately, but it's also about being ahead of the curve. It means buying before the curve starts to trend upwards, and selling before it starts to trend downwards. And the upward and downward trends will be partly driven by what the others are doing. So they need to be responding faster than the competition. My financial services client has elephants who are very good at what they do, in analysing and, in this way, mitigating risk.

But they also need tigers who can respond intuitively and quickly, based on a limited and selective use of information and signals, to be ahead of the curve and the competition.

Tigers enjoy working with variability

As we have seen, variability is at the heart of risk. We also know that the world would be a dull place without variability. And we are somehow conditioned to want to do something about that variability – to work with it and, at the same time, against it.

Imagine a game of tennis where the ball bounced in exactly the same place and to the same height before you hit it. You would master the game very quickly by playing pretty much the same shot every time. You might become very good at it, but how interesting would it be? Why don't they make golf courses with all the holes the same length, in a straight line with the same size greens, and the hole in the same spot on each of them? You can see the point. We enjoy the variety, but at the same time we are honing our skills to try and counteract that variability; that we hit the same quality of tennis shot regardless of where it bounces and how high; that the golf ball heads towards the green regardless of the distance we are away and what type of ground surface we are hitting it off.

It's as though life is designed to create risk, and then deal with it, either by going with it, or working to counteract it, and that is part of how we enjoy life.

While the elephant mindset is, to some extent, that variability is an annoying distraction, for tigers it's part of their reason to exist. In fact, tigers are naturally anti-fragile, according to Taleb's view of risk (*Antifragile – How to Live in a World We Don't Understand*, 2012). His proposition is that we as individuals and organizations are naturally fragile within the uncertain world in which we live. The market can change due to new technology; our lives can change due to an unexpected illness or accident. And we tend to respond by doing things to compensate for this fragility by trying to create robustness. We diversify by investing in other products with other technologies in other markets. We cut costs to save money for that unforeseen event, and we take out expensive insurance to cover eventualities of various kinds. And somehow it still doesn't seem to bring the peace we seek.

Taleb proposes an alternative model – anti-fragility. It's a kind of working *with* the variability and risk, rather than against it. He takes part of his cue from nature. Plants work through a process of death being the source of new life. Part of the fruit or flower of the plant, a seed, is deliberately disconnected from the plant and is buried – and this is what creates new life. Or the cutting of a branch through pruning creates an environment for even more vigorous growth than was there before.

> *The best way to verify that you are alive is by checking if you like variations ... Food would not taste if not for hunger; results are meaningless without effort, joy without sadness, convictions without uncertainty; and an ethical life isn't so when stripped of personal risks. (Taleb N. N.,* Antifragile: How to Live in a World We Don't Understand, *2012)*

Our human bodies are built to be anti-fragile – clearly designed to deal at least as much with the consequences of risk as to be able to avoid it. Wounds heal themselves with relatively minimal outside help, and white blood corpuscles fight off unwelcome bugs which are part of the risky external environment that our bodies inhabit. Our health systems seek to create robustness which is a pale comparison to the anti-fragility that is part of our human make-up.

Taleb's arguments apply the lessons of organisms such as plants and the human body to human organizations. Those that try to create systems to constrain risk, by having checks and balances at every corner, will never be as effective as anti-fragile organizations that work with risk, where every part of that organization is designed and motivated to take a risk situation and do something better as a result of it.

The biggest constraint, he argues, is the agency problem, which will be developed more in Chapter 12 when I talk about organizational character and alignment. We don't behave like anti-fragile organizations because our individual risk profiles are so different from those of the organization with which we are engaged. How often does doing something to protect or recover a position in our own organization actually lead us to greater personal risk?

Organizational leaders could benefit so much from learning how to get more from their people in their natural capability to deal with risk.

They could also benefit from understanding more about how human bodies are designed to live with and deal with risk.

This happens not just at a psychological level, but also at a physiological one.

Physiological factors

We learn from John Coates in his intriguing book *Hour Between Dog and Wolf* (2012) that risk is a 'whole body' experience. Coates was formerly a financial trader in New York, and then switched careers to become a medical practitioner based in Cambridge in the UK. His extensive research looks at how humans respond to risk physiologically, that is, through the production and delivery of hormones.

It appears that three hormones play slightly different roles when we are confronted with situations involving some element of risk: cortisol, adrenaline and testosterone. These hormones respond to variable inputs to the body: visual input through the eyes, a sound, a smell or even some kind of impact to our skin's sensory nerve endings. What is interesting then is the role that the brain has in processing this information, and how the hormonal system is tied to that response.

Coates observes that in sport, for example, the speed of response needed by a player reacting to an approaching tennis or cricket ball, and making a skilful connection with that ball suggests that normal brain-based analytical processes can't be too heavily involved. There isn't the theoretical time for the information to be sent to the brain, processed and sent back to the muscles that need then to respond. It would appear that some kinds of pre-conscious and rapid communication between brain and muscles are what actually keeps us alive in fast-moving situations. Hormones have some kind of role in facilitating this, even though they themselves don't move that fast. Separately, conscious reflection shows up later, to analyse what has happened.

From this, we have the concept of muscle memory. I am a keen tennis player, and am only too aware of the importance of muscle memory. It works for you and against you. Against in the sense that for most of my life I have not been hitting shots with a top spin action, which requires a loose wrist. My muscles remember a firmer wrist and flatter shot, and my mind is trying to convince them otherwise. But it works for me in that once I have practised it a few thousand times, my mind doesn't have to keep reminding my muscles what to do when I am playing in a match. And that's important when the ball is hurtling over the net onto my end of the court, and I need to react both quickly and accurately.

In the case of tennis, you wouldn't typically refer to this kind of muscle memory as 'intuition'. But Coates observed something very similar, and quite mystifying, on the financial trading floor. Traders, it would appear, seem to develop muscle memory for responding to situations, even before they have very much information, and certainly before they have much time to analyse it. He tells stories of traders sensing a buzz on the trading floor, or even change of tone of voice here and there, or the speed at which information was appearing on the screen and issuing a 'buy' or 'sell' order immediately.

Speed, once again, in financial trading is of the essence. Being even a couple of minutes slower in executing a trade can make huge differences in financial returns. The trading floor is really a place for tigers – elephants need not apply!

Malcolm Gladwell gave us his take on intuition in his book *Blink* (2006). He claims that you can extract as much value from 'the blink of an eye as you can from months of rational analysis'. He draws from a wide range of experiences ranging from medical decisions to reading facial expressions.

The testosterone winner effect

What is even more intriguing to the interplay between risk and strategy is what Coates calls the winner effect. And it's all down to testosterone. This is based on the study of animals, where winning a fight increases the likelihood of winning again, independent of any other variables such as natural strength or size. Scientists in trying to explain this phenomenon noticed a pronounced rise in testosterone levels as male animals in particular prepared for a contest. The testosterone has anabolic effects on muscle mass and haemoglobin, producing quicker reaction times and increased persistence and fearlessness. What is interesting is that after the fight is over, the winning animal emerges with higher levels of testosterone than the losing animal. This makes some sense in a typical animal world – the losing animal disappears to nurse its wounds while the winner needs to prepare for the next challenge.

Coates believes this same winner effect is evident in humans, having run tests at sporting events such as tennis competitions. Wins will raise testosterone levels, which in turn increases some of the attributes needed to improve the chances of winning again. This of course is not helpful for athletes who are not winning, but Coates has suggestions about other aspects that can also raise testosterone, such as intense rivalries and home advantage. He suggests the examples of Ayrton Senna and Alain Prost in Formula One racing, Muhammad Ali and Joe Frazier in boxing, and John McEnroe and Bjorn Borg in tennis.

So we see in another way why winning brings risk into the heart of strategy making. If and when risk is a whole body experience, and strategy is about addressing a winning aspiration, one clearly must feed the other. The tigers in the team, or even the tiger within us, not only can feed us with helpful intuition, but also can bring a winning physiology to improve our chances of winning again.

Do we see evidence of this in leaders making strategic decisions? We probably can't make a strong scientific case, but there does seem to be a sense that this is true. Once scientists like Isaac Newton make one breakthrough discovery, they seem to go on a roll towards others. Once Napoleon had achieved one victory through Strategic Intuition at Toulon, he then continued towards many other military victories.

Once Steve Jobs had achieved innovation fame with the Macintosh, there was something in his winning physiology that led him to serial innovation successes.

Is the ongoing growth and expansion of Virgin all to do with a powerful brand, or some core business competences that somehow translate into all kinds of different business sectors? Or is there something in the physiology of Richard Branson that doesn't know how to be defeated?

What makes you come alive

John Eldredge writes in his book *Wild at Heart* (2001) about an 'adventure to live' that inhabits our souls, particularly those of men. His thesis is that we only truly embrace life when we embrace risk as the theme of our lives. He claims that a person won't truly be happy until they have adventure in their work, and he remembers advice that he was once given:

'Don't ask yourself what the world needs. Ask yourself what makes you come alive, and go do that, because what the world needs is people who have come alive'.

He argues that we are in constant danger of not being the actors in the drama of our lives, but instead the reactors 'to go where the world takes us, to drift with whatever current happens to be running the strongest'.

My hypothesis is that there is a tiger in each one of us that intuitively knows what risks to take, but a tiger that needs the elephant in us to guide us from the risks we should avoid. To help us work that out, one thing I believe is helpful is being more aware of some of the traps that can catch us out. In a sense, these are sort of 'games of the mind'. This is the subject of the following chapter.

Chapter 7

Games of the mind

In this chapter, I will examine the factors that can impact on how we evaluate and respond to risk. In our research, we referred to 'illusions', and concluded that both the formal 'elephant' mode and the informal 'tiger' mode of working with risk are susceptible to illusion. There is a whole body of recent literature from mathematical psychologists such as Daniel Kahneman and Nassim Taleb that addresses the illusions and framing effects that can influence our perceptions.

We cannot think holistically about risk without considering some of the ways in which our views about risk can become distorted or irrational, when we presume that they are rational. This is important not just in helping us to make confident decisions, but also in how we engage with and influence others who may see things differently. In this chapter, I look at the following ways that illusions can be created:

• risk management
• risk compensation
• black swans and turkeys
• confirmation bias
• cognitive inertia
• loss aversion
• probabilistic biases (e.g. Bayesian)
• statistical graphical illusions
• broad framing

Our research highlighted the idea that both the analytical elephant and the intuitive tiger approaches come with health warnings, illusions and framing effects that can distort decision making without us realizing it. Let's have a look at some of these issues.

Risk management

First of all, the main issue with the formal elephant approach is that risk management is in a sense an illusion. There is an implicit idea that with the right processes, you can somehow manage away uncertainty. Or that leaders can somehow delegate risk to specialists, and no longer need to be concerned about it. Even where there are several layers of risk responsibility, starting perhaps with the line manager or relationship manager (as in the case of banking), through to the Head of Risk, and finally through to the Risk Committee, there is a sense that someone else is dealing with it, so that you don't really need to.

It's similar to the classical issues with quality management through Quality Control teams. As long as you have one of these, quality is their problem and not yours. I am aware of a case of an insurance business that was facing problems with the quality of its claims handling. It had a quality checking department, but this clearly wasn't picking up all the errors before the documentation was sent to the client. So they decided to try and fix this by creating two further points in the process where quality was checked. The level of incidence of errors went up. When consultants investigated why this was happening, it was clear that each quality checking point assumed that it didn't need to be that thorough, because one of the other two would surely pick up any errors. And the level of attention to detail actually declined.

So there is an issue of shared or even delegated responsibility feeling like 'passing the buck'. But on top of that, some kind of formal process to evaluate risk suggests that risk can be put in a neat little box and told to keep quiet. And while this may help, it has its own risks.

When we considered risk as variability, and considered all the variables that could conspire together to deliver an adverse result, or even a crisis, one thing we notice is that there are a lot of them. Some of them are fairly complex – not least human behaviour.

During our research into risk at Ashridge, I spoke to a director at the Financial Services Authority, before it became the Financial Conduct Authority. He talked about the shortcomings of a massive computer model designed to calculate bank risk across the industry. Its main aim was to avert the risk of bankruptcy and avert crisis. Well, in 2008, it clearly didn't work. It was a sophisticated model, but in his view it didn't, and couldn't, account for the complexity and variability of human behaviour. As we know, econometric models tend to assume rational human behaviour, but there aren't any humans who actually behave like that, as we shall explore further in the coming pages.

Risk compensation

A by-product of the illusion of risk management is that if we think risk has been taken care of, we start to behave in irrationally risky ways. So in a sense, the more risk management we put in place, the more risk we take. This may of course be deliberate in terms of wanting to encourage more risk-taking behaviour, or it may simply undermine the purpose of the risk management approach.

There is in fact a recognized psychological phenomenon known as Risk Compensation or Risk Homeostasis. This is the idea that people typically adjust their behaviour in response to the perceived level of risk, becoming more careful when they sense greater risk, and less careful when they feel more protected. An example of this is that passive safety systems in cars, such as seat belts and anti-lock braking, can cause motorists to drive faster.

There is a sense that this manifests itself in an apparently growing risk appetite. The more risk we take, without realizing a negative outcome, the more we believe that we can take. In a sense, our risk appetite compensates for past risks successfully taken. So we see this in serial entrepreneurship. A successful record business for Richard Branson makes the risk of taking on British Airways in an airline business seem less daunting. Success in airlines makes entering mobile telephony and finance feel less risky. Ultimately, and amazingly, once you've done all that, even running trains on a major UK route seems like a manageable risk.

We can tell similar stories when it comes to progressing from personal computers to music to mobile telephony to mobile money; risk successfully taken has a compensating dilution effect on perceived risk going forward. These examples show that risk compensation can have a positive impact; but sometimes past success can have an unhelpful anaesthetic impact on perceived risk in the future. Such is the case when we think about Black Swans, cognitive inertia and confirmation biases, covered in the following sections.

Black swans and turkeys

As we have seen, the formal approach to risk management works with the idea that risk is based on variability, and that we can often model this variability around a normal curve, where variability is the standard deviation of expected outcomes. This clearly works best where we can measure multiple outcomes from multiple decisions of a similar nature, as we can, for example, when tracking financial trades. And we can look at historic performance and make the assumption that that gives us a reasonable guide for what could happen in the future.

So this formal approach to risk modelling is largely based on the idea that the world will continue to behave in the way we have observed it to behave up to now. Nassim Taleb captures the shortcomings of this thinking in his famous book *The Black Swan* (2010). The story is that until recently, based on historic observations, many would have argued that 'all swans are white'. And this proved to be a useful guide for predicting the colour of the next set of swans we would meet, or indeed spotting them on a lake from a distance. This was fine until someone discovered some rare black swans. Now we have proof that the theory 'all swans are white' is not true. And we are now not quite as sure of the likely colour of the next set of swans we meet.

The Black Swan is a metaphor for an extremely unlikely event, and one that nobody expects to meet.

Taleb also talks quite amusingly about the turkey's eye view of the world, which is that life is for the long run involving eating, resting and generally clucking around. Our 'helicopter' view of turkeys, however, is that they are for eating at Christmas or Thanksgiving, after a short period of rearing. The turkeys' experience never prepares them for the one extreme event at the end of their lives but we know that it's not that extreme.

This is why, in Taleb's view, models based on normal curves don't work, as they don't take account of the fat-tailed extreme events, which may not actually turn out to be that extreme.

As I write this, we have just heard about the resignation of Volkswagen's CEO, Martin Winterkorn, as a result of the emissions cheating scandal concerning the company's US diesel cars. This is a classic case of a Black Swan event, one for which it would have been hard to plan or predict. In terms of financial returns to shareholders, this becomes a massively negative number as the share price dropped to nearly half what it was before the scandal. It does indeed threaten to be a fat tail to the left of the normal curve.

The big question with the Black Swan is, can you – and if you can, should you – plan for such an outcome? Should such outcomes become a factor in planning the strategy?

Taleb claims that successful businesses are precisely those that know how to work around inherent unpredictability and even exploit it. He also points out that some Black Swans are positive. This is particularly true of the movie business (and indeed many publishing businesses), where most of the time you achieve somewhere between a marginal positive and a marginal negative return, but every now and then you get a blockbuster hit. Venture capitalists operate on similar principles: invest in ten ventures, many fail, but one will be a phenomenal success.

Taleb proposes that, because of Black Swans, businesses should invest in 'preparedness' not 'prediction'. He argues that what you are really interested in is not how likely it is to happen, but the consequences if it does. He says all you have to do is have a contingency plan for the consequences.

While I see the merit in this thinking, I am not overly convinced that we can or should plan for any and every eventuality. There are times when contingency planning may be counterproductive. Yes, having enough lifeboats on the Titanic, in the rare eventuality of coming across a Black Swan iceberg, probably makes sense. But there may be times when 'burning the ships', as practised by Hernan Cortez (see Chapter 5 on mitigation) so that the men have to stay, fight and survive, is the right thing.

Taleb's concept of anti-fragility is one way in which to address the Black Swan issue. I will explore this in more depth later on in the book when I consider organizational character in Chapter 12.

Confirmation bias

This is the idea that our beliefs make it difficult for us to be objective and unbiased about any evidence which might contradict them. And it's a fundamental issue in decision making.

It's a particular issue with science, and the inductive method of reasoning, which seeks to develop general theories from specific observations. The theory stands as long as the observations support it. But as soon as the evidence no longer supports it, the theory is no longer valid – it has been falsified. So the theory can never be proved, but only disproved.

Karl Popper was one of the leading philosophers of the twentieth century, and known for his views on science, encapsulated by the idea that 'there are two kinds of scientific theory: ones that have been falsified and ones that haven't been falsified yet'. In addition, he argued that only science that could be falsified was useful for discovering truth, and that falsifiable theories that were less probable and therefore more 'risky' were more useful than those that were probable but couldn't be falsified. He tended to categorize much social science as the latter.

So we have the example of the theory 'all swans are white' as useful but easily falsifiable, as you only have to discover one black swan. So Popper argued that striving to find ways to falsify your theory is good science – and he associates Einstein as a leading proponent of this approach: as his 'riskier' theories were being falsified through his own experimentation, he was constantly looking for a better theory to explain his observations.

But the problem is that this goes against human nature. Effectively we need to ask, what piece of evidence would we most expect to see if what we believed to be true is not in fact true?

Take a couple of simple tests to illustrate. I give you a sequence of three numbers that follow a general rule, and the exercise is to work out what that rule is. To help you, I then ask you to suggest other sequences of three numbers, and in response to each I tell you whether or not they meet the rule. If my rule is that the sequence of numbers are in ascending order, people generally find this difficult to get. Why? Because they are looking for something more sophisticated. However, they will keep suggesting sequences which are in line with the rule and this doesn't help them get closer to the rule. The way to discover the rule is to suggest sequences that don't follow the rule. But we don't naturally do this because of confirmation bias (Goodwin & Wright, 2004).

Try another experiment. You have four paper cards with one of the characters D, R, 4 and 6 on the faces of the cards that are showing. The question is which card should you turn to confirm or deny the rule that 'if a card has a D on one side, it will have a 4 on the other'. Normally, people chose the D and the 4, but turning over the 4 doesn't help at all, as anything on the other side will not disprove the rule. On the other hand, if you turned over the 6 to reveal a D, then that would disprove the rule.

A close relative of this issue is that of cognitive inertia.

Cognitive inertia

Cognitive inertia, sometimes referred to as cognitive dissonance reduction, is similar to confirmation bias in that our ability to evaluate a situation objectively, or to come up with new creative solutions, is adversely affected not only by our beliefs, but more particularly by decisions we have already taken. For example, cognitive dissonance occurs when we encounter evidence that conflicts with a decision that we have already made and it feels uncomfortable, so we try to minimize that dissonance. As a result, we tend to find it hard to evaluate the new evidence objectively or rationally. This can affect both risk averse and risk taking behaviour, and I will illustrate this with examples of each.

Let me invite you to spend a few minutes with the Game Show Host conundrum. Try and do this without looking at the answer below, because your response to the answer is important. Then assuming you have completed the exercise, now read on.

This Game Show Host conundrum demonstrates cognitive dissonance reduction. It has become viral on the internet and led to heated debates between professional mathematicians, partly in my view because it demonstrates cognitive dissonance so well. Try this:

1. On a game show, contestants are asked to pick between three doors. Behind one of the doors is a prize. As a contestant, you select one door. The Game Show Host then opens a second door, one of the doors you didn't pick, deliberately to reveal that the prize is not behind that door. You are then asked if you would like to switch your choice to the last remaining door. What do you do?
   a. Stick with your original choice?
   b. Switch your choice to the remaining door?

Now consider this scenario:

2. This is repeated ten times, with the prize moving randomly between the doors; and you get a much bigger prize if you pick the prize more than five times. Each time the same thing happens, you pick a door, the Game Show Host opens a second door without a prize, and you get a choice as to whether to stick or change your choice. What do you do?

   a. Stick with original choice every time?
   b. Switch your choice to the remaining door every time?
   c. Mix up both sticking and switching options?

THE ANSWER: Having selected your choice for both scenarios, I will now tell you that the majority of respondents answer 'a' in exercise 1, and 'a' and 'c' about equally in exercise 2: most do not switch doors. But I also need to tell you that you double your chances of winning if you change your choice, you have a 2 in 3 chance of winning if you switch doors, compared to a 1 in 3 chance of winning if you stick with your original choice.

   While this may not make intuitive sense, and indeed a number of professional mathematicians don't accept this outcome, you can prove it by doing a simulation with a friend a number of times with three cards (with an Ace as the prize). Ask a friend to pick a card, then show them a second card which is not the Ace and ask if they would like to switch their choice to the remaining card. If you do this 10 or 20 times, you will begin to see that by switching to the remaining card, your friend would win the prize 2 times out of 3, whereas by sticking, they only win 1 time out of 3.

This is a metaphor for cognitive inertia, and illustrates something interesting about our intuitive approach to risk. And it's a double whammy – it happens in two ways.

Firstly, the idea that we have already picked a door (i.e. made a decision) makes it more difficult for us to consider changing that decision. This is the first level of inertia. But to switch doors increases our chances of winning, that is, it reduces our risk of losing. So the change option is actually the low-risk option.

Secondly, there is a much more pervasive form of inertia where we justify our decision based on our own assessment of probability. Most people think that they have a 50:50 chance whether they stick or switch, so why switch. Interestingly, the inertia dissipates slightly in the second multiple attempt scenario, with a proportion of respondents going for the mix'n'match approach. But what happens when I explain that actually the odds are twice as good if you switch? Normally, the initial reaction to that piece of news is 'You're wrong!', rather than 'So how can you show me that that is the case?'

It is fascinating that there is, or at least was, an internet site with this problem and solution set out, and a blog of commentary from supposedly leading mathematicians arguing quite vociferously that this is not true, that the odds do not improve or that this is bad mathematics. And yet, as I suggest, you only need to run it as a simulation enough times to convince you of the pattern, to see that you do indeed double your odds. So it's an illustration of how hard it is to stand back from decisions and hard-fought beliefs, and to look at something from a different perspective.

Goodwin and Wright (2004) give an example of the issue of sunk costs in the Tennessee-Tombigwe water project connecting Tennessee to the

Gulf of Mexico. Apparently, about US$1bn was spent on the project before an assessment was made that the cost to complete from there was greater than the benefits to be realized. What was the response from the leadership on the project? 'To terminate a project in which US$1bn of taxpayers' money has already been invested represents an unconscionable mishandling of taxpayers' dollars'. The story of the Anglo-French Concorde project was similar, with only twenty planes ever built at a cost also of around US$1bn. There were very few orders, but the project was allowed to continue for many years in spite of likely failure because of money already spent.

Campbell et al. (2008) have some great examples of this kind of cognitive inertia in decisions which, while high risk, turned out to be reckless. Smithburg, the chairman of Quaker, had witnessed the success of the product Gatorade, and decided that the company should take the risk to acquire another similar product. He acquired a product called Snapple at very high cost, but because the characteristics of this product were actually very different from those of Gatorade, it failed and ended up bankrupting the company. The success of Gatorade created a belief system that was hard to unpick objectively.

Another interesting case which Campbell et al. cite is that of Operation Market Garden in the Second World War, as captured in the film *A Bridge Too Far*. The strategy was to capture three strategic bridges in northern Europe, at Graven, Nijmegen and Arnhem. The mission failed: Arnhem could not be captured without a heavy cost of life. There were personal agendas amongst senior generals, Browning and Montgomery, which were distorting the decision-making process. Eisenhower wanted to be more cautious, but was persuaded otherwise. How much did the success of the D-Day landings only months before play into the decision-making process, and create a belief that 'boldness pays', that was hard to evaluate more objectively?

In these instances, cognitive inertia has fed into greater risk taking, which turned out to be reckless. But it can frequently have the opposite effect. Beliefs we have about our marketplace, or our ways of doing things that have been developed over years, can dull the antennae that pick up the need to change. In the case of the collapse of Kodak, the belief that they were a chemical company and that there *must* be a future in chemistry-based photography was one that was hard to change. In their case, the risk of not changing clearly did outweigh the risk of changing.

Lateral thinking

There is something about dissonance with beliefs that is picked up by the practice of lateral thinking, popularized by Edward de Bono (1999). What gets in the way of thinking laterally about problems are the subconscious assumptions that we make without realizing it. There are certain kinds of solutions that are naturally unavailable to us because we have already written them off.

In many of the cases I have just described, this is partly what is going on. In the Game Show Host problem, for example, there appears to be an underlying assumption that if I am now looking at the option of selecting one of two doors for the prize, my chances of getting it right with either selection is 50/50. How can what has happened already up to this point have any bearing on my odds now? Somehow, the past cannot be relevant.

For Smithburg at Quaker and the generals at Operation Market Garden, something different was happening. There is an underlying assumption that there is something inherent in previous successes which must be repeatable. There is a subconscious assumption that somehow there is no need to look too closely at a new set of variables, as why should they be any different from the previous set.

One of my favourite lateral thinking problems is the one where a man and his son are in a car accident. The man is killed, and the son is rushed to hospital. At the hospital, the surgeon announces, 'I cannot operate on him because he is my son'. How can this be? Often people wrestle with all sorts of subtle explanations: the man came back to life; the surgeon is talking figuratively; it's a dream, etc. There is a very simple explanation, which can make those who've missed it feel quite annoyed – the surgeon is of course his mother.

Why does this happen? Today, women are doing most jobs that men do, including being surgeons. And yet many people struggle with this particular scenario because at a subconscious level, they believe a surgeon must be male. The point is we are not being obstinate, and refusing to change our beliefs or assumptions, although this clearly does happen. We genuinely struggle to remain or become objective when making decisions about things where we cannot know everything there is to know.

I think this is what often happens with risk. We assume it's about bad news, so we don't really want to talk about it; or somehow that exploring it might make it more likely to happen. Or we assume the opposite – that somehow bad things cannot happen to us. Either way, we are like ostriches with our heads in the sand, the idea being that if we don't look, then the bad thing won't happen. Or we become like Teflon, convinced that nothing bad can stick to us. Either way we are elephants, and believe that ultimately analysis and sound thinking are the only valid ways to work with risk. Or we are tigers, and we believe that trusting our gut instinct is really the only honourable way to make decisions.

I really love this lateral thinking issue. It's not that it provides the answers to this conundrum that is part of our humanity, but I do think it starts to ask the right questions. Later on I talk about 'Intelligent Ignorance' in more depth – getting the right questions. With these lateral thinking problems, once you get the right questions, then the answers fall out quite quickly. 'Are we making assumptions about the gender of the surgeon?'

Lateral thinking is one of the underlying themes of this book. If I'm an elephant, then all tigers are crazy. If I'm a tiger, then elephants are unenlightened. What if those assumptions are wrong? As de Bono (1999) stated, what if the answer is neither 'yes' nor 'no', but 'po'?

So we have started to unpick some of what might get in the way of working well with risk. There's more. What else? Let's have a look at loss aversion and framing effects, and tap into some of the wisdom of Daniel Kahneman and friends.

Loss aversion

Cognitive inertia has a cousin who also tends to distort our ability to evaluate risk objectively: loss aversion.

Daniel Kahneman, with his colleague Ivan Tversky, won a Nobel Prize for their work on risk studied from a mathematical-psychological perspective, which they called Prospect Theory. They showed that our approach to risk is not symmetrical – in essence, we would generally prefer to avoid a loss than to achieve a gain.

This was brought home to me quite vividly at an Olympics legacy event where we had Cath Bishop, a former rowing silver medallist, answer a question about how much the glory of winning motivated her to go on and win more – she responded that the pain of losing, having previously come so close, was much more motivating. Cath stated in a subsequent email to me:

> *Reflecting on it, for me, failing and losing was extremely painful but valuably set in train a vital process of rigorous, open, honest and fairly brutal self-analysis and analysis of the wider team and training environment in order to learn the lessons that were then vital to turning things round and using that experience to come back better, stronger and faster thereafter. Success was impossible for me without losing and learning the hard lessons of losing that I needed in order to get to the higher level required to win. And the emotions of defeat were harsher and seemed to linger longer than those of success.*

Kahneman talks about what he calls 'Framing' effects. This is the extent to which how a problem is described can influence our assessment of it, and therefore our decision. Let's look at this exercise in more detail (see the box below).

Dilemma No. 1. You are the health minister for a country that is preparing for the expected outbreak of a disease, which is likely to kill 600 people. You are advised of two programme options to combat the disease. Programme A is guaranteed to save the lives of 200 people. With Programme B, there is a one-third probability that 600 people will be saved, and a two-thirds probability that no one will be saved. Which of the two programmes would you favour?
a. Programme A – save 200 lives
b. Programme B – one-third probability of saving 600 lives, and two-thirds probability that no one is saved

Dilemma No. 2. You are the health minister of a country that is preparing for the expected outbreak of a disease, which is likely to kill 600 people. You are advised of two programme options to combat the disease. With Programme A, 400 people will die. With Programme B, there is a one-third probability that nobody will die, and a two-thirds probability that 600 people will die. Which of the two programmes would you favour?

a. Programme A – 400 will die
b. Programme B – one-thirds probability that no one will die, two-thirds probability that all 600 will die

The point of this exercise is that both sets of options are in fact the same choice; they are just framed differently. You may have answered both the same, as you can see both together and consider the implications of each carefully by comparison. When Kahneman and Tversky ran the original experiment, they had two large groups, one of which was given the first scenario and the other the second scenario. What they found was that in the first, the majority went for option A, while in the second scenario, the majority went for option B. Their conclusion was that this was because the framing encouraged the option that least referred to loss. In the first, option B spoke more of the *possibility* of loss; in the second, option A spoke more of loss.

Understanding loss aversion is part of the recipe for being influential as a leader. It's one of the reasons, in my view, why some of the persuasive selling techniques don't really work. If no attention is paid to what they might lose, emphasizing the benefits in terms of what someone can gain can often miss the mark. The former tends to have a lot more sway over the 'buying' decision.

As a coach I see this pattern repeated frequently. We reach a point in the conversation where it becomes clear to my coachee that the best course of action is to confront the issue head-on – to have that tough conversation. It all makes sense; there's just one small problem: there is a slight risk of losing their job. This is particularly true in environments where jobs are being lost in redundancy programmes – and there appears to be more and more of those. That loss aversion ultimately drives many decisions in organizations, and affects its culture and character. I will look at this in more depth in the later chapter on organizational character.

Broad framing

This then brings me onto another framing effect, broad framing, which can have a big influence on how we tackle dilemmas involving risk, and which often have an ethical dimension. This statement in the box by Paul Polman, Chairman of Unilever, is an example of broad framing. It sets the scene for issues we will tackle later around how we set the aspirations for the organization, and the longer-term potential impact on business.

Kahneman (2011) introduces the concept of broad framing in his book *Thinking Fast and Slow*. He talks about being offered better than even odds on the tossing of a coin: say, put down £1,000 and receive £2,000 if you win. Many of us would hesitate on a single coin toss – they would be different amounts about which we would hesitate, depending on our personal wealth and general risk of 'broad framing' appetite, but there would be a point we would logically all freeze. In the film *The Gambler*, there is a scene when the gambler, played by Mark Wahlberg, takes all his extensive winnings from a long session of Black Jack, and puts them all on a single bet on the red at the roulette table. It's a moment that gives you a bit of a sick feeling: it's all or nothing in one go. This is narrow framing!

What Kahneman then says is that if we were offered the same deal for ten coin tosses, that is, 2 to 1 return on a 50/50 probability bet, most of us would take it – we are almost guaranteed to win! This is broad framing. It is what keeps financial market traders sane. If they lose badly on this trade, they know they will make it up on others.

In the Game Show Host problem, the reason I ask people to consider Question 2, which involves repeating the exercise 10 times, is that in this case, it is much clearer that switching is better over 10 iterations.

When I run this exercise live with participants, I run it 10 times. If I only do it once, I cannot be confident that it will show that switching was the right way to go. But when I do it 10 times, switching tends to produce the winning result either 6 or 7 times out of 10 – that is, reflecting the 66 per cent chance of winning, compared to the 33 per cent chance if you stick with your original choice. This demonstrates broad framing.

And this is a useful metaphor for how we approach risk in business decisions. If we just look at in the here and now, we have a distorted view. When we take risks, we may lose in the short term. But if we are broad framing, we are looking at the longer-term odds – the bigger picture. The Paul Polman quote below is interesting to me, as it sets a new tone for a major organization like Unilever. The key word for me is 'ultimately', in terms of *when* shareholders should expect returns from this new social emphasis. There is a risk that, taken to heart, this vision could prove to be costly. There could be a decline in short-term shareholder returns; such is the nature of risk. But he has placed his bets on the long-term view.

Our modern slavery research presents a conundrum for the retail organizations to whom we are talking. There are clearly risks in tackling the issue within a highly complex supply chain. There are risks that the costs to do it properly in the short term will outweigh the returns, and profitability will decline. There are risks of supply chain disruption, as supplier relationships have to be terminated, and products then become either unavailable or more expensive to buy. There are risks that the collaboration that is needed to deal with it effectively, as different retailers deal with the same overseas suppliers, will undermine competitive advantage – and may even lead to problems with anti-competition legislation.

> *The great challenge of the 21st century is to provide good standards of living for 7 billion people without depleting the Earth's resources ... and ultimately this will result in good shareholder returns ... It is an enormous learning curve as no one has been trained for this.*
>
> Paul Polman, Chief Executive, Unilever (Confino, 2012)

But the broad framing of this issue proposes that a global supply chain that treats workers fairly will become a more effective supply chain. That ultimately it will be good for business. Not only that, but it leads to a more harmonious world. It proposes that businesses such as Unilever that are developing an increasingly social agenda can realize some of their ambitions in this way. It suggests that business becomes the catalyst for positive social change in the parts that politics has failed to or cannot reach.

The group effect

What happens to our approach to risk when we get together to discuss things is a key theme in this book, as we start to explore organizational character. The answer to whether we become more or less risk averse is that it depends on the character or culture of the group. If concerns about discord are high within the group, or there is a strong 'be perfect' lead in the group, then this can tend to reduce risky behaviour. However, if the group character is one that encourages challenge and creativity, then there can be an opposite effect – the group can move towards higher-risk behaviour because any risk is effectively shared.

Two different models describe these two situations. One is described as 'Groupthink' and works something like this.

> A small highly cohesive management team faced with a decision dilemma is likely to become so concerned about group solidarity that individual deficiencies in information processing and decision making will be magnified. Groupthink is then essentially the suppression of ideas that are critical of the direction in which a group is moving. It is reflected as a tendency to concur with the position and views that are perceived as favoured by the group. (Goodwin & Wright, 2004)

However, an opposite effect called 'Risky shift' was explored in studies by Stoner (1967) in the 1960s and showed that 'the decision made by a group will be riskier than that of the average individual member'. Several hypotheses have been proposed to explain the phenomenon. The prevailing one is that dominant cultural values influence the decision and that these values become more salient in group discussion.

Another explanation is that when individuals engage in group discussion, they change their positions so as to be more extreme than others in the group, resulting in the shift.

These appear to be two opposing views as to whether seeking to collaborate in a group in a decision-making process will increase or reduce risk appetite. One factor appears to be the culture or character associated with the group, a feature I explore in more depth in Chapter 12.

Logical illusions

Logic is not all that it seems to be. Most of us think we are fairly logical, but it's perhaps surprising how often it can trip us up. Our assessment of probability can often be flawed, even though we think we are quite rational. Try answering the question in the following box.

Class Birthday Problem

In a class of thirty people, what is the probability that two people celebrate the same birthday (i.e. same day of the year)?
a. Less than 1 per cent
b. Between 1 per cent and 5 per cent
c. Between 5 per cent and 50 per cent
d. More than 50 per cent

Most people answer between 1 per cent and 5 per cent. But the answer is (d). In fact, it's over 70 per cent, but I don't put that as an option because I think people would anticipate that it's a really unlikely outcome, and pick that; such is the oddity of human psychology. It is actually very likely that two people in a class of thirty have the same birthday. If you're not convinced, then there are ways to simulate it using a spreadsheet, or just try it with post-it notes or something next time you're in a group of that size.

The science of probability can be surprising. In fact, I find randomness intriguing in itself. The paradox of randomness comes to life when you consider the following point. When you are doing research, how do you check for randomness? One way is to pick a measure such as height when researching people; if you get a normal distribution of height, it's a strong indication that your sample is random. So in other words, the way to test for randomness is whether your result follows a very precise pattern. Odd, eh?

Sample size is also often a challenging one. If you do research with a completely random sample of only 50 people across the UK, you can predict the reaction of the 50+ million people in the UK to a pragmatic level of accuracy – say of the order of ±20 per cent depending on what you are measuring. The key is ensuring the sample is randomly selected, which is not as straightforward as it may sound. But given that, the surprising result is that if, for example, you ask a random group of 50 UK adults to name their favourite soft drink, and 30 per cent say Coke, the highest response, and only 20 per cent say Pepsi, the next highest, you can be pretty confident that Coke is the nation's adults' favourite soft drink. I know people get confused about this, and ask why political opinion poll sample sizes are in the thousands. The reason here is that they have to be very accurate because of how our political system works. A small percentage difference in the polls can have a large impact on the overall election result, as it can be the difference between whether a whole load of marginal seats are won or lost. And even then, it isn't always a good predictor for all sorts of other reasons (e.g. difference between stated intent and actual actions).

One of the other probability areas where people get caught out is in the Bayesian problem.

Bayesian effects

One of my favourite 'one line' jokes goes like this: 'Did you know, I am more likely to be mugged in London than I am in New York. [Pause for effect] ... That's because I hardly ever go to New York'.

This is an example of Bayesian probability. In the nineteenth century, the Reverend Bayes came up with a formula for calculating the results of conditional probability. Put more simply, that is what happens to overall likelihood when you combine two types of variability. So in our joke example, we have the variability of getting mugged in either London or New York, and the variability of the amount of time I spend in either London or New York. So given I am in New York, my likelihood of getting mugged is, say, 5 per cent, whereas, given I am in London, my likelihood of getting mugged is, say, 1 per cent. However, I only spend 10 per cent of my time in New York, and 90 per cent in London. So overall the chances on any given day that I am mugged in New York are 0.5 per cent (5 per cent × 10 per cent), whereas the chance that I am mugged in London is 0.9 per cent (1 per cent × 90 per cent) – that is, London is higher than New York.

This might sound like a trivial example which doesn't matter that much, but I believe we can see Bayesian confusion created by authoritative voices in society, particularly when it comes to medical issues. Taleb picks up on this particular example in *Fooled by Randomness* (Taleb 2007). You have a disease which can affect 1 in 1,000 people (i.e. 0.1 per cent), and the test for the disease is 95 per cent accurate, which means there is 5 per cent false positive. That means that in a sample of 100 test results, five of those will indicate a disease which isn't there. If someone gets a positive test result, what are the chances they actually have the disease? Many would say 95 per cent. Actually it's much lower: 2 per cent. That's a surprise to many of us. This is how it can be explained. In a random group of 1,000 people, all who happen to have been tested, only one probably has the disease. However, of the remaining 999, about 50 (5 per cent of 999) will have tested positive for the disease. So out of that 50, the chances that you are the one that have the disease is 1 in 50, that is, 2 per cent. This is quite a powerful illusion. I wonder how many people who have been tested for a fairly rare disease with what appears to be a fairly reliable test, and testing positive, have been told there is a high chance they have the disease.

Visual illusions

One of the most pervasive concepts we have when thinking about strategy under uncertainty is that it is getting more difficult because change is just happening more quickly. So we tend to be more likely to conclude with Error Type B (see Chapter 2), there is no point in making decisions because the chances are very high that we will have to change them in a little while, when something else big happens to change everything.

You will have gathered by now that I don't support this view. I believe we do need to be prepared to make tough choices as leaders, even though they can entail significant risk. Now comes perhaps one of the more radical ideas in this book:

> *I'm not totally convinced that change is actually happening faster now than it was in the past.*

There: I have said it. Partly, I wonder if it's the basis for not making decisions which, as leaders, I believe we are often paid to make. I wonder if it's a bit of a cop-out.

I am also aware that there is a growing body of business people who have a vested interest in the idea that change is happening fast. It is the fundamental calling card for management consultants, of which I am one and have been for much of my professional career. So with this kind of vested interest, I naturally feel a tad suspicious that the very same people are the ones promoting the idea that 'you'd better watch out, because change keeps accelerating'!

There is one example of where I am aware of an illusion that helps to promote this idea. It is the illusion that our population has been growing faster in recent decades than it has been throughout the history of mankind. And it is captured in a graph that looks something like the one below (Figure 7.1). The headline is 'here is another example of how much change is accelerating in the last hundred years or so'. The reality is that this curve is the output from a mathematical model of population growth. The rate of growth actually remains the same throughout the time period represented by the x-axis – that is, as shown here, since the beginning of time. The main driver of population growth is the average number of offspring per couple who then go on to reproduce themselves. If this growth factor is above 2, population grows; if it is below 2, population declines. In this model, this growth factor is actually the same throughout the time period represented. Population growth is not actually accelerating; the rate of sustainable reproduction has remained the same throughout the time period.

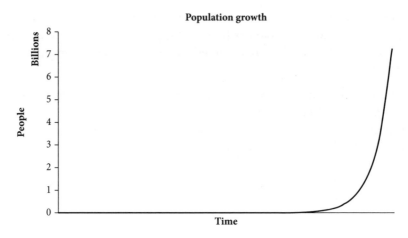

Figure 7.1 Illusion of rapid change

Game theory and collaboration

We cannot really get to the bottom of risk in strategy without consider-ing game theory. Morgenstern and Von Neumann (Leonard, Von Neumann, Morgenstern and the Creation of Game Theory, 2010) pioneered this science, building on the study of chess. John Nash devel-oped the thinking at Princeton, winning the Nobel Prize for his work on the subject of equilibrium.

The Prisoner's Dilemma is probably the most famous example of game theory. In brief, two prisoners are each offered the choice to betray the other, as a key witness to the other's guilt. The outcome for each pris-oner depends both on what they do, and what the other does. If both talk, they both get a fairly severe punishment. If one talks and the other keeps quiet, the betrayer goes free while the other gets the most severe sentence. If both keep quiet, they both get some punishment, but not as severe as if they both talk. The idea is that ideally, if you have any insights into how the other prisoner is likely to behave, this determines your optimal choice. However, in the absence of that, you are left with a higher risk option and a lower risk option. The lower risk option is considered the one that has the least worst possible outcome for you – sometimes referred to as Minimax. That means you minimize the maximum loss you can experience. Interestingly, in the Prisoner's Dilemma, this is the one where you talk, and is therefore the competitive option. You are talking and hoping the other prisoner doesn't. Not talking, which could be considered the more collaborative approach, is actually the higher risk option. That is because if you don't talk and the other prisoner does, this is the worst outcome for you. But if you both keep quiet, you both end up with the second best outcome.

It is curiously counterintuitive that a combative approach, effectively a pre-emptive strike, by the prisoner that talks is actually the lower risk option. It feels more risky. But in a sense, this is aligned with our research Pointer that change can seem risky, but not changing may be more risky. When it comes to innovation, there's risk if you do and risk if you don't. As in the case of the Game Show Host, switching is the 'lower risk of losing' option, or the higher chance of winning.

So when it comes to competitive pre-emptive strike, what happens to Nash's collaborative equilibrium? There clearly is a place for this, where opposing parties are able to work something out, which is sub-optimal but good for each. The Prisoner's Dilemma suggests that this is the more risky course of action. Collaboration is risky. But it can be the right risk, and I will argue through this book, it often is. It's more likely to deliver a longer-term solution; it is more likely to work out if we can 'broad frame' what we are looking at.

When you run the Prisoner's Dilemma as a game over successive rounds, what tends to happen is that if both players don't talk and achieve a reasonable although sub-optimal result, this tends to stabilize. The players quickly learn to trust each other. Once one has talked, then subsequent rounds can tend to oscillate between talking and not-talking options, with each at different stages achieving maximum and minimum outcomes. It is hard to recover the position of mutual trust where neither player talks.

So game theory suggests to us that collaboration can be the higher risk option in the short term but, as stability sets in, the lower risk in the longer term.

Chapter 8

Aspiring to win

Now that we have explored the nature of risk, how we work with it differently and how we can be fooled by it, I would now like to return to the premise I developed in the opening chapter. Good strategy means being choiceful about taking risk – it's about taking the right risk.

This begs the question, how do we know what the right risk is to take? I believe there are a number of factors that can contribute to the answer to that question. One of them has to be the purpose of the organization. This will not only be the anchor which sustains our pursuit of the right strategy, but it will also define our approach to risk. This is particularly true if we define our purpose as a 'winning aspiration'.

Strategy is associated with the idea of winning. And it's the winning aspiration that ups the ante in terms of risk. If you want to win, you need to be prepared to take appropriate risks.

The word 'strategy' is derived from the Greek word for military leader, *strategos*, and has its origins in military combat, where there is generally an enemy and the objective is generally to beat that enemy. Achieving this is considered a successful outcome, and often described as victory or winning. Conversely, failing to achieve this is generally described as defeat or losing. It is interesting that for most (but not all) military combat throughout history, it is clear who has been victorious and who is defeated; who has won and who has lost.

Strategy as a concept has been adopted by the business world, largely because most business involves a certain level of competition. In intriguing contrast to military combat, since Adam Smith outlined the essential elements of an effective global capitalist marketplace in the *Wealth of Nations*, first published in 1776 (Smith, 1997), competition, a 'battle' against some kind of opposition, is considered to be a good thing and fundamental to the working of the capitalist model.

Smith made the case that 'people of the same trade' meeting together was likely to end with 'conspiracy against the public' and in a 'contrivance to raise prices' – which formed the basis for today's anti-competition legislation. The implication is that healthy competition is good for customers as it keeps prices of goods down, and encourages increased efficiency of production.

So by having competition, we have the concept of winners and losers, although in contrast to military conflict, defining a winner and a loser is less clear-cut in a competitive marketplace.

Nevertheless, businesses have adapted to the concept of a strategy as a way of thinking about how to do better than the competition. Why? Because this typically leads to a more profitable business, which in turn generates funds to re-invest to make the business even more profitable. And so it goes around.

One of the best known books on strategy, and still extensively taught in business schools today, is Michael Porter's *Competitive Strategy* (1980). By implication, it sets strategy in the context of competition. His basic thesis is that a business creates a competitive advantage by 'deliberately choosing a different set of activities to deliver unique value'. When I was completing my MBA at Wharton Business School in the early 1980s, it had only just been published and was seen as a brilliantly insightful view of how to conduct business successfully. It was regularly referred to in the various cases that we covered during the course. Competitive advantage was all about how firms can be more likely to 'win' in their marketplace. As individuals and teams working competitively on cases, we were also keen to win, as this generally led to better grades – and ultimately a 'winning' mindset pervaded everything.

In my view, one of the best recent texts on strategy is jointly written by A. G. Lafley, the CEO of Procter & Gamble (P&G) between 2000 and 2009, and Roger Martin, the Dean of Rotman School of Management. They both have connections with Porter's strategy firm, Monitor Company; Martin worked there and was involved in advising P&G on strategy. Their book is called *Playing to Win: How Strategy Really Works* (Lafley & Martin, 2013), and draws some of its case examples from a very successful period at P&G. During the period from 2000 to 2009, while Lafley was CEO, P&G's sales doubled and profits quadrupled; the share price increased by more than 80 per cent during a period when the S&P 500 index declined overall. This seems like a good definition of winning in an economic marketplace, although it does not overtly address the performance of the competition, and who the losers were.

Lafley and Martin talk about strategy as an 'integrated set of choices that uniquely positions the firm in its industry so as to create sustainable advantage and superior value relative to the competition'. So in their eyes, the winning is about sustainable advantage and superior value, however we might measure these things. They state quite provocatively: 'what matters is winning' and that 'winning should be at the heart of any strategy'.

I would like to explore at least, and possibly even challenge, the idea that 'what matters is winning'. I think it has merits, but also needs to be treated with some caution. And I would like to develop this further in the remainder of this chapter.

A winning aspiration creates a need for risk

But for now, if we accept 'what matters is winning', then it is this aspect of strategy more than anything that defines the need to take risk. Lafley and Martin go on to talk about what they consider ineffective approaches to strategy, which are driven by a 'reluctance to make truly hard choices'.

What makes tough choices tough is risk. We don't know for sure that they will lead to the desired outcome, and in making these choices, we are exposed to the possibility that we may have got it wrong. But the premise is that we can't win if we don't make those choices or if we don't take that risk. It's only by exposing ourselves to the potential downside that we can achieve the upside.

This is a risk to the organization, and it's also a risk to the leader or leadership group making those choices. Lafley and Martin propose that 'the world needs more business leaders who understand strategy and are capable of leading the strategy process for their companies...it requires clear and hard thinking, real creativity, courage and personal leadership'.

This links with the 'Bold Creative' character attribute from the Blonay Character Profiler. It links with Jim Collins's (2001) findings that leaders in the top organizations in his research, arguably the winning organizations that outperformed the financial market averages by several multiples, needed resolve as one of their attributes. It links with Treacy and Wiersema's assertion that market leaders, winners even, need to be bold enough to focus on one of the disciplines – Product Leadership, Customer Intimacy or Operational Excellence – and not try to be all things to all markets.

Lessons in risk from sport

While strategy draws from military combat as its metaphor, our best metaphor for winning must surely be sport. When Lafley and Martin talk about playing to win, and choosing to win and not just simply playing, as someone who is passionate about sport, I think of sport. I think immediately of those rather boring football matches that gave the distinct impression that both teams were just 'simply playing'. They were primarily defensive, not wishing to concede a goal, and happy in the end with a draw. Many years ago, the football authorities set out to address this malady by awarding three points for a win instead of two, and only one for a draw. So they skewed the odds in favour of risk taking. It seems to have fixed it to some extent, but you still see a surprising amount of defensive safe play. It's the old loss-aversion problem kicking in. Psychologically, even though you are more likely to reach a rewarded position in the league (promotion to the next division, European league football), you have the sense that players still have an asymmetrical preference for not losing, rather than winning.

But the successful teams have a different attitude. Manchester United, for example, at least in their successful years, were known for their passion for winning, as reflected in their more attacking, more risk-taking approach to the game. Alex Ferguson, in his autobiography, talks about the 'attacking' risks in the closing quarter of an hour of the game to seek to ensure they won. They became well known for winning games in the closing minutes. It didn't always work – such is the nature of risk. But over a season, it paid dividends.

I always took risks. My plan was: don't panic until the last 15 minutes, keep patient until the last quarter of an hour, then go gung-ho ... No team ever entered Old Trafford thinking United might be persuaded to give in. There was no comfort to be gained from thinking we could be demoralised. Leading 1–0 or 2–1, the opposition manager would know he faces a final 15 minutes in which we would go hell for leather. That fear factor was always there. By going for the throat, and shoving bodies into the box, we would pose the question: can you handle it? On top of our frantic endeavours, we would be testing the character of the defending team. And they knew it. Any flaw would widen into a crack. (Ferguson, 2013)

Let's look at another rather different example of how the desire to win can impact the approach to risk.

My game is tennis, and I notice that an approach to risk is being played out on a point-by-point basis. An approach can be planned in advance, in the form of an overall match or set strategy, but in reality you have a point strategy, or even an in-the-moment shot strategy. So how does risk manifest itself in tennis? Well, one way is in the approaches to the net as shown in the following diagram (Figure 8.1). This is based on some fairly rough and ready research of rally length and outcomes in professional games. The average rally length in a game is around a surprisingly low five shots total, so 2.5 per player. In terms of winning or losing shots, at the top professional level of the game, this is split very close to 50:50 – it's surprising how close a lot of professional games are in terms of points won or lost.

So what does this chart show us? This is an equivalent to a normal distribution curve for two types of tennis shot: the darker left hand bars represent the distribution for shots played from the back of the court, and the lighter right hand from the net area. There are just three points in the distribution for each shot type, as we are only interested in three possible outcomes from the shot; either it's a winning shot, it's a losing shot, or the rally continues so that the player gets another shot.

So first to note that our flatter 'curve' is our more risky shot, remembering the way I demonstrated risk and variability in the earlier chapter. In

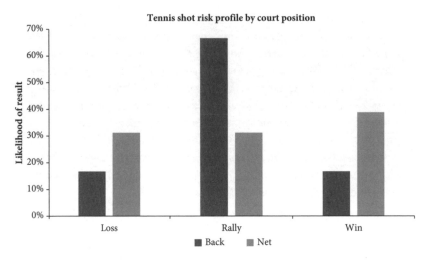

Figure 8.1 Analysing risk in tennis

other words, there is more variability in possible outcome with our flat-ter profiled (lighter shaded) net shot – which is what we would expect. The net shot is more risky; there is more chance of the extreme outcomes, either a win or a loss.

A back-of-the-court shot is less risky; it has a more peaked profile – the most likely outcome from the shot by a good margin is a continuation of the rally.

So what we see from this is that the shot which has a higher chance of winning the point is the shot at the net – that is, the more risky shot.

What is interesting is that tennis players know this, and yet the shot at the net is a relatively rare part of the game at the professional level today. It used to be more regularly played; up until the late 1970s and early 1980s, the serve and volley at the net was a regular way for players to win points, particularly on grass courts. Of course, there are a number of reasons why that has changed. Tennis balls are slower and make it harder to hit winners. The perfected top spin ground shot, pioneered by Bjorn Borg, changed everything, making it easier to hit dipping passing shots. And longer rallies and games mean energy is a bigger factor – coming to the net expends more energy.

However, the most interesting feature of this analysis is one other reason why us tennis players are more reluctant to come to the net. Yes, there may be a higher chance that the shot will be a winner. But there is also a higher chance it will be a loser. And, in the tiger moment, away from rational elephant analysis, our loss aversion kicks in!

Victory calls for risk

When we look back to the military metaphor, one of the better known moments of winning aspiration was encapsulated in Winston Churchill's speech to parliament in the early stages of the Second World War. 'You ask, what is our aim? I can answer in one word: Victory'. He defined victory in terms of the protection of British style civilization as we know it. He described the alternative of a Dark Age under Hitler. He painted a picture in the future of a history book headline which would read: 'This was their finest hour!' And in doing all this, he inspired a nation to risk all for the cause. In all of the aspects we hear about the way we approached this war, boldness, courage and resolve were probably the most dominant characteristics.

It seems this idea of creating a vision of winning for future memories, such as Churchill's 'This was their finest hour' quote, is at the heart of the military metaphor to encourage risk taking. Shakespeare's Henry V, in his motivational speech prior to the Battle of Agincourt, calls on his men to consider that as a small 'band of brothers' ready to shed their blood for a great cause, they shall be remembered for generations to come. Henry V was known to have taken significant risk at Agincourt, not least facing the French at all and being outnumbered by potentially four to one. A number of key decisions turned out to be right risk decisions: his choice of battlefield, his decision to attack first and then lure the French into the path of the technically superior long bows, his choice of lighter armour while the French heavier armour caused them major problems in the mud and the confined space they had between two woods. We see in Agincourt the combination of winning vision and deliberate strategic choices which is a recurring theme in our study of risky strategy.

This story shall the good man teach his son... but we in it shall be remembered; We few, we happy few, we band of brothers; for he today that sheds his blood with me shall be my brother... and gentlemen in England now abed shall think themselves accursed they were not here p 434. (Shakespeare, c 1599) King Henry V Act IV, Scene 3

The combination of courage and single-minded focus on victory became a major inspiration to the idea of military strategy during the time of the Napoleonic wars. With the development of new technology in more sophisticated artillery at this time both at sea and on land, warfare had become more complicated and demanded better thinking and planning. This was seen particularly clearly in the military victories of Napoleon Bonaparte, witnessed from a distance by a certain Carl von Clausewitz, who is probably the best known military strategist through his work *On War* (1976). Clausewitz wrote: 'War is the Realm of Chance'.

Clausewitz is one of the main inspirations behind a book on military strategy written by Colin Gray, a professor at Reading University, who writes in his book *Fighting Talk* (2009) that the reason that chance has a major role to play in war is because of its complexity. He talks about the strategic gambler, striving to reduce the risks. He states that: 'The more extreme the stakes, the greater should be the effort to mark the cards in one's favour, yet the more difficult that must prove to be. Risk-free warfare is not an option'.

We see examples of the combinations of highly disciplined focus on a goal and bold resolve in the accounts of Napoleon's victories. We shall look in more detail in the next chapter at how Napoleon worked with risk so effectively.

We see similar traits in his naval rival Horatio Nelson. We learn from Jonathan Gifford's *History Lessons* (2010) that Nelson was prepared to disobey orders if his instincts told him that the route to victory lay elsewhere.

Risk in bold adventures – the race to the Pole

Turning from the military metaphor to that of the bold explorer, we see an intriguing relationship between 'winning' and 'risk' in the race to the South Pole in 1910, between the English Robert Falcon Scott and the Norwegian Roald Amundsen. For both explorers, winning was, at least in part, about being the first to reach the South Pole, one of the last unexplored areas on Earth. For both, this undoubtedly involved a high level of personal risk, to themselves and their chosen teams. But this is where the similarities end.

Amundsen reached the Pole first, and returned to his ship with a team completely intact. By contrast, Scott arrived at the Pole weeks later; he and his entire team failed to return alive.

What else was different? Firstly, their specified goals were different. Amundsen had a single goal: to be the first to reach the South Pole. It was probably the best example of a clearly defined and focused winning aspiration – easy to confirm or measure success. Scott had two goals: to get to the Pole first, like Amundsen, and to gather scientific information about the Antarctic. As a result of this, they each took different types of risks.

Scott, with his dual goals, in a situation where time was a critical factor, delayed on his return trip to collect geological samples, which also added weight to his sledges. Amundsen, on the other hand, took a different kind of risk, which was consistent with his winning goal. While Scott chose a route from McMurdo Sound, which had already been partly explored by Ernest Shackleton in 1907, Amundsen chose an unchartered route from the Bay of Whales, which was on the edge of the Great Ice Barrier, where explorers had feared that the ice could fracture and send you floating away. But Amundsen chose this because it was 60 miles closer to the Pole. In addition, because Scott believed that Amundsen would choose the same route as him, he also assumed that he, Scott, was ahead of him, as there were no signs of Amundsen's tracks. With this assumption, he had no compelling drive to go faster.

However, in this amazing story, even though Amundsen's single-minded winning goal led to certain risks, he compensated for this by reducing risk in other ways. He had investigated the records of other explorers who had been in the area, and noted that the ice had remained unchanged for decades. So this gave him more confidence in his choice of routes.

Amundsen had also researched the best type of transport to use by spending time with the Inuit Eskimos in the Arctic. He used dogs that were very well suited to the extreme conditions. Scott, on the other hand, for most of the journey used a combination of ponies, motor sledges and man-hauling. The motor sledges were untested and quickly broke down. The ponies, although they could haul heavier loads than dogs, were also ill suited – they had no natural vegetation to feed on, sweated through their hides which led heavy ice to form and caused them to sink more deeply into the snow. Eventually all of the ponies had to be put down. This left man-hauling for most of the journey, recommended by Shackleton to be the best and most noble approach. But a noble but ill-conceived approach didn't get the job done.

What this famous piece of history tells us about winning and risk is that while a winning aspiration creates the need and appetite for risk, leaders need to be choiceful about which risks they take, and which ones they work hard to avoid.

Winning and the Olay story

Lafley and Martin (2013) tell the story of the successful relaunch of Oil of Olay by P&G, which took it from a failing US$800mn dollar business in the late 1990s to a US$2.5bn market-leading business with high margins by 2010. This came as a result of extensive research, which led to re-positioning the product to appeal to a younger population and new technology to create a range of benefits for this target group. They also created a new category in health and beauty for their sales channels, which they called the 'mastige' category. This straddled both the mass retailers like Walmart and the prestige retail of department stores – an upmarket offer in the former and a more competitively priced offer in the latter. And to encompass the range of technologies covered, the 'Oil of' was dropped and it was branded just as 'Olay'.

This was an illustration of a core part of P&G's corporate strategy – to develop leading brands in the categories in which it competes. It believes that it needs to do this to achieve one of its overall winning aspirations, to 'meaningfully improve the lives of the world's consumers'. In turn, its strategic process is a cascade where the corporate strategy becomes a 'winning aspiration' for the brand – so, in the case of Olay, to become a leading skincare brand in the channels and markets in which it chooses to compete.

So to win was defined corporately in terms of meeting a range of social needs for the world's consumers. There might be something of a question as to how you know whether you have won or not at this level. However, at the brand level, this was translated into leading the competition – becoming the leading brand in the category. The language in both cases is the same. The language of winning cascades down throughout the organization, from beating competition in the market to having the best most efficient processes to support that.

Lafley and Martin say: 'Strategy is about making specific choices to win in the market place.' They say there is a need for more leaders who understand strategy and the processes which support it, in government, healthcare, education and what they call the social sector. They say it requires 'clear and hard thinking, real creativity, courage and personal leadership'. Turning this around, to win you need to make specific choices, and this requires courage – it means taking risk.

They talk about McDonald's winning aspiration as: 'Be our customer's favourite place and way to eat'. There's nowhere to hide there if you're the second favourite. Nike's mission is perhaps even bolder: 'To bring inspiration and innovation to every athlete*in the world (*If you have a body, you're an athlete)'. So is there anyone on the planet not experienced and been inspired by Nike? Again, there's nowhere to hide with a statement like that. This might have something to do with the apparent success of these two organizations.

Lafley and Martin conclude: 'Winning is worthwhile; a significant proportion of industry value-creation process accrues to the industry leader. But winning is also hard. It takes hard choices, dedicated effort, and substantial investment'.

Competing or collaborating

So strategy tends to be about winning, and winning means taking risk. It generally means competing – that is, having one or more opponents. It derives its thinking from military thinking – which is first and foremost about beating the enemy.

But is that really what business and organizational life should be about? Is a strategy that just focuses on winning really all that helpful? Most businesses are also involved in collaborating in their markets with other organizations, as partners or in customer supplier relationships. Sometimes there is even collaboration with competitors. How does that impact strategic thinking? What impact does that have on risk thinking?

My brief exploration of game theory in the previous chapter suggested that collaboration may produce longer lasting benefits. Looking at our organizational mission through a broader frame can lead us to conclude that collaboration is more optimal than competing. But that somewhat counterintuitively, choosing a collaborative path may actually be a higher risk option in the short term.

My Ashridge colleague Eve Poole wrote the first title in this series of Ashridge Business Books, of which this book forms a part. Hers was entitled *Capitalism's Toxic Assumptions* (2015), in which she makes a compelling case for why a number of aspects of capitalism may be unhelpful for society, and unpicks some of Adam Smith's (1997) original thinking. I agree with a lot of it, yet I have mixed views about the first subject she tackles: the need for competition. Essentially her view is that competition as a default position is essentially unhelpful, and that collaboration is a much better approach. Adam Smith's idea is that businesses should compete with each other, otherwise they would conspire to raise prices unreasonably to the detriment of the public, meaning customers. International anti-competition legislation, as well as the work of the Monopolies and Mergers Commission, is based on this premise, and has been a thorn in the side of major successful organizations such as Microsoft and Apple.

Eve argues that collaboration can lead to a much more efficient use of resources, to everyone's advantage, and I think there is a strong case for this. In the research we are currently conducting with primarily major UK retailers to tackle modern slavery in their global supply chains, collaboration is an important idea. The supply chains are complex with multiple tiers of suppliers, and the problem is generally well hidden. There is often a criminal element which specializes in not being discovered. The solution is not just about exposing it, but in helping suppliers to have the capacity and the right approach to overcome it – to be able to continue to operate efficiently without the abuse of human rights.

This requires a significant investment in resource by the UK retailers that we are working with. And it only makes sense to operate in collaboration with competing peer organizations, as in many cases they are working with the same suppliers at some level in the supply chain. This avoids duplicated effort by suppliers, already in many cases either struggling or reluctant to co-operate. And the influence of multiple retailers is clearly greater than that of a single retailer.

But this collaboration creates a tension in a business for which the normal mode of operation is to compete head-on with the very same players in the marketplace. The supply chain can be a prime source of competitive advantage, an advantage that can be quickly diluted once they start to collaborate. For one of our participants, there was a visceral response in the board room when she mentioned that she was working in a group which included their arch rival – largely responsible for bringing them to the brink of failure. Collaboration of this kind can strike at the very heart of a business's DNA.

It also creates problems for the lawyers and anti-competitive legislation. Competing retailers should not be talking to each other about anything. Ironically, our research has been triggered by the UK Modern Slavery Act being passed into law in the spring of 2015. So what we have now is two different pieces of business-related legislation that are competing with each other at some level, at least at the symbolic level of 'you must not share information' versus 'you must share information'.

There is a bigger picture that is perhaps emerging here. We are increasingly concerned about human rights across our planet, and wanting to eliminate poverty and pay a 'living wage'. One way to help achieve this, and I believe the best way, is to prioritize fair employment. Where necessary, businesses should collaborate to help achieve this. But our capitalist mindset tells us to prioritize the customer, and encourage competition to help achieve this. The world's well-treated customers are predominantly in western, developed economies. The world's poorly treated employees are predominantly in developing countries. Is it time to revisit the priorities? How radical would it be to stop saying 'The customer is king', and start saying the 'The worker is king'. How helpful could this be in changing what we teach in business schools, and beyond?

So I agree with Eve's views on the challenge to our assumed competitive positioning. However, I think there is still a place for a sense of competitiveness and a desire to win, and I know she would also agree with me on this. There is something fundamental in our human spirit that responds well to the desire to win. And where this creates helpful, motivated, even collegiate behaviour, this seems to be a good thing. The irony is that we probably collaborate best and most enthusiastically in seeking to overcome some kind of common opposition. We are probably more prepared to take the right risk when we share this winning aspiration.

In the case of the collaboration that is needed to address global issues such as workers' rights and modern slavery, our risk-taking, competitive mindset still needs a winning aspiration, and probably still needs an opposition to be defeated. Our opposition to fair working practice globally is perhaps the immoral and even criminal behaviour of the profiteering 'middle men', whoever and wherever they might be. Or it could be the apathy of a developed world public who seek primarily to maintain or better their current welfare, regardless of others.

Sport combines competing and collaborating

Another colleague Cath Bishop, Olympics rowing silver medallist, has a particular view on the importance of tempering a competitive mindset with effective collaboration. The story she tells me is as follows:

I experienced different 'competitive environments' through my rowing career – one regime for one Olympiad I trained in was a hugely competitive yet very negative environment where we were pitted against each other daily, and another's gain was seen as your loss (an overtly zero sum gain mentality), and where only a few rose to the top and performed, and many were burnt out and the vast majority of the squad underperformed at the Olympics. During my final (and most successful) Olympiad, we were again of course in a competitive environment, but it felt very different – another's gain, i.e. another athlete beats you in a training session, was seen as a positive for everyone, a sign that the programme was working, that standards were going up, that you were part of something bigger than you that was successful and that you could and should aspire to reach that new standard set and raise it yet further – in this environment, everyone reached higher standards and got closer to their potential, and hadn't been burnt out by daily competition against each other before getting to the Olympics where you then need to compete against and face the 'real opponents'.

Cath is a speaker on effective leadership from a sports perspective, building also on her experience of working in the British Foreign Office, where competitive behaviours are rarely conducive to winning outcomes. She also talks about the New Zealand rugby team, who do not spend a lot of time developing 'competitive' behaviours amongst the team, as that would be destructive. Instead, they recognize that it's more important to bond, to encourage and support each other and achieve your best individual and team performance levels, in order to be able to go and be competitive against the rest of the world when it matters.

Clearly an assumption that we can draw on all our competitive metaphors from sport to demonstrate that competition is the only way to encourage a winning mindset would be wrong. It's the balance between the two, holding the two in healthy tension, which is the key. In the same way, the right risk is a choiceful affair, not cowardly but prudent, not reckless but courageous.

We can look at the example of Dave Brailsford, who masterminded famous cycling victories in the Olympics and Tour de France, who is both a great team builder – essential in the field of cycling – and a famous risk taker. One thing that is well known is his relentless pursuit of 'marginal gains', a keen attention to the factors that can make all the difference in the heat of the moment. This requires a good awareness of the variables which are most likely to impact winning or losing. At the heart of knowing which risks to take is understanding variability – which means the effective synthesis of information.

Chapter 9

Synthesis and key variables

So we set the case for risk with a 'winning aspiration', then we are faced with the question of where to risk or where not to risk. This is where it is helpful to view risk in terms of variability. A strategy that is oriented towards a winning aspiration is risky because of the variables that can either help or hinder the winning cause. A key step in knowing where to take risk is understanding what are the really important variables which can impact the cause, and find ways either to reduce variability, or work with it.

The problem is that there are often too many variables, and we can quickly get bogged down in analysis paralysis, or oversimplify to the one or two variables with which we are most comfortable.

The classic example of oversimplification is where we consider entering a new market with a new product, and decide that all we really need to do is research potential customers, to try and predict their behaviour when offered our new proposition. They tell us that in 20 per cent of cases they would accept it, so we predict that our market share will end up as 20 per cent. It doesn't work out like that because we've failed to take account of a few key variables: how competitors will react, whether the channels to market will work with us, and at what cost, what is happening to the economy and the level of disposable income, new emerging technologies that will substitute for our proposition, and so on.

When I teach business school students about these kinds of variables, we draw on models like:

a) PESTEL: a summary of trend variable types categorized under the headings Political, Economic, Social, Technological, Environmental, and Legal; and

b) Porter's Five Forces: direct competitors, new entrants, substitutes, suppliers and customers.

What typically happens in the exercises is that students research these variables as associated with their cases, and report back on a plethora of data, with some attempt to work out the implications of their findings. Where they tend to struggle more is in breaking their analysis down into the two or three things that will really make a difference.

The challenge is in synthesizing the information. This is about working out which of the variables will make all the difference. Good strategic decision makers need to be able to do this, but it's an art as much as a science. It's as much about intuition as it is about analysis. It needs tigers and elephants to get together. Elephants can get bogged down in the detail. Tigers can fall into the trap of picking their favourite variable, and assuming it will behave in the same way that it did before.

When I look at the realm of combat strategy, I notice that military risk-taking leaders often appear to have a talent for determining what risks to address, or more specifically, what variables to focus on.

We know that Napoleon took risks to achieve victory. But we also learned that he did a lot to avoid unnecessary risk. He famously had an amazing capacity for remembering certain aspects of detail. He developed a good understanding of the behaviour of his enemy – for example, he researched how the British fleet had responded in different military encounters in recent history. He understood the dynamics of the key tools of his trade – he knew artillery, and what it could and couldn't do, and how accurate it was. His view of the range of possible results of these variables informed his strategic choices. Someone who studied Napoleon before delivering one of the best known studies on military strategy was von Clausewitz.

Friction, gaps and variability

Another way of thinking about variability is to consider von Clausewitz's concept of sources of friction that can impede effective implementation. Stephen Bungay (2011) refers to this when he talks of the three types of gaps between strategy making and effective action:

a) The Knowledge Gap: the difference between what we would like to know and what we actually know.

b) The Alignment Gap: the difference between what we want people to do and what they actually do.

c) The Effects Gap: the difference between what we expect our actions to achieve and what they actually achieve.

In my view, these gaps are a good summary of the variability that is associated with implementing strategy. In effect, according to our variability definition, they are one way of looking at the risk associated with strategy. When I initially talked about variability in Chapter 4 (Section 'Risk as variability'), I listed a whole range of variables in a 'variable tree'. Human behaviour was one of those, and is one which affects all three of the gaps. Most specifically, employee or follower behaviour is the primary variable playing out in the Alignment Gap. Human behaviour has a role to play on both the Knowledge Gap and the Effects Gap, whether that is customer behaviour, competitor behaviour, investor behaviour or whatever. Then there are more extreme forms of human behaviour, such as criminal or terrorist activity.

Finally, there are a whole range of non-human factors that contribute to both our Knowledge and Effects Gaps: geography, the weather, how technology actually behaves, or the onset of illness and disease.

These are all variables that impact the effectiveness of strategy, and therefore should be taken into account when deciding what is sensible to plan for, and more importantly, how we organize to implement strategy. This is Bungay's point, and therefore impacts how we think about organizing, the ability for organizations to adapt to variability and the devolving of decision making to enable this to happen.

But I have argued that good strategy making should seek to address these variables head-on. This can be done either by reducing their variability through mitigating strategies, which may indeed mean that we create organizational flexibility and devolve decision making. Or it may mean that we take the risk, we take on the gamble with eyes open, knowing the odds, selective in what key bits of information or signals we trust, and trusting our intuition.

Let us look in more detail at Napoleon's strategy at the siege of Toulon, the victory which catapulted him to political as well as military leadership in a highly volatile France. As already stated, he had studied and was an expert in artillery. So he knew the variables that affected artillery performance and he had studied the behaviour of his enemy, the British fleet, which had occupied the port of Toulon in a bid to support a counter-revolutionary movement within France. In particular, he knew of the British fleet's recent activity in the American War of Independence and had a sense of how variable and indeed predictable their response would be. So he formulated a strategy at Toulon that took account of these variables, and his intuition that it would work was strong enough that he gave a firm command. He knew about the variability of behaviour of his men – and knew that personally leading the assault would reduce that variability. His aim was to remove the British fleet from Toulon. He didn't say to his second-in-commands 'Now come up with a combination of different attacks to achieve that aim'. That had already been tried. He didn't even say, let's put artillery on a hill – you go and pick which hill. He didn't even say 'Let's stick a few guns on that hill and see what happens'. He knew that by gaining a foothold and putting artillery on a specific hill, the British fleet would leave Toulon. And he turned out to be right. There was a clear specific strategy, and an equally clear and emphatic outcome.

Interestingly, his enemy, Nelson, was remarkably similar. Nelson in particular made a point of studying the weather – an important variable to understand manoeuvres at sea. He also understood the difference in capability of his ships compared to those of the French and Spanish, and the geometry of ship combat. So at Trafalgar, he knew that the weather conditions were perfect for a radical departure from traditional sea combat at the time. His ships approached the enemy ships head-on, rather than the usual broadside-to-broadside approach. In one sense, the variability of possible outcomes was huge because this was an untried strategy. And as his ships approached the enemy, they could effectively only receive fire and not deliver it. However, once they were astern the enemy ships, this situation was reversed. All their guns could fire on the enemy ships at close quarters. The range of accuracy of the guns, another significant variable in broadside to broadside combat, was now effectively taken out of the equation. Firing at any range was almost guaranteed to hit an enemy ship. We know that strategy worked. Trafalgar was a great victory for the British fleet, which effectively halted Napoleon's war efforts to gain supremacy of the seas, and was probably the beginning of the turnaround of fortunes in the Napoleonic wars. Nelson understood the key variables well, and developed a strategy on that basis. He took the right risks, although ultimately he lost his own life in the process, arguably the ultimate personal risk.

Steve Jobs at Apple understood the variables in the computer market well. Early in the life of Apple, he had witnessed positive customer behaviour in the original Apple PC, and not such positive customer behaviour with the failure of Lisa. When he saw the Icon and mouse-based user interface technology developed by the Palo Alto Research Centre, he came up with a strategy to adopt that technology whole-heartedly. It wasn't a case of setting an aim to win in the personal computer market, and letting loose his generals to come up with different ways of doing that. He made the decision. He understood the variables. He trusted his intuition and took the risk to launch the Apple Mac. Interestingly, he clearly had less understanding of the vari-ability of senior management behaviour, and subsequent actions meant arguably he took the wrong kind of risk with them – at least in the short term. In the longer run, he was able to come to understand that variable better, and return to working with the risks he under-stood the best – continuing to make clear strategic decisions, prioritiz-ing design, taking on the music industry, tackling the phone market and so on.

Understanding and working with variability, as a manifestation of risk, seems to be somewhat of an art, reserved for tiger-like leaders such as Napoleon, Nelson and Steve Jobs, who trusted their intuition above all else. But I will explore how this would be a misrepresentation of what actually happens. I will look in more depth how these kinds of leaders have a mix of elephant and tiger, executing a formal analytical approach and an informal intuitive approach, respectively.

Before I do that, I would like to take a closer look at how we can adopt a more formal approach for different ways of looking at variability, a way of developing 20:20 vision.

20:20 vision

So the riskiness of our strategic decision making will be heavily influenced by our ability to predict the future, which in turn is affected by the level of variability of factors that matters to us.

Courtney writes about 20:20 vision (2001) as developing a thorough understanding of the uncertainty that you face. He argues that it is only when you have done this that you can make sensible strategic choices, and he also outlines some generic choices, which I will come back to. He has a particularly neat way of looking at this. He talks about four levels of 'residual uncertainty', which is what is left after you've done the research and the analysis. It's the uncertainty or degree of variability that is left once you know all there is to know. Of course, this in turn begs the question, how do you know what you know? For an elephant, this is clearer than it is for a tiger. So for now, we'll assume, as I believe Courtney does, an elephant approach to this:

- **Level 1** is a clear single-point view of the future, where there's a high level of confidence (e.g. likely value of an appreciating property if I buy now);
- **Level 2** is about alternate futures that have two characteristics. They are both 'mutually exclusive' and 'collectively exhaustive'. This is borrowed from a favourite McKinsey choice selection tool with the acronym MECE, named after two properties to describe a limited set of discrete options. 'Mutually exclusive' means that no one option overlaps in what it covers with any other option. You cannot have a bit of both options. 'Collectively exhaustive' means that the options together cover all the available space of where you could go. Examples of useful MECE models of the future are: Which technology standard will prevail for video cassettes, VHS or Betamax? Basically they were the only two games in town; both could not realistically co-exist for long. Alternatively, what is the identity of the next president of the USA?
- **Level 3** is about a defined range of futures. Typically, planners will try and pick a representative set for scenario planning. For example, the future market demand for broadband, based on what has happened so far, is likely to fall within a certain range. A number of variables

such as technology development and economic health will have an impact on this range. Sometimes the range can be unhelpfully wide, and of course it is important for the strategist to be aware of this. So in the early years of the century, forecasters were estimating that the global market for jumbo and superjumbo planes could be 1,500 units over the next twenty years or as little as 350. Lehman Brothers predicted that Airbus would need to sell 528 superjumbos to break even over that time period. This made for an interesting and informed strategic discussion, which needed to understand the level of risk in any major investment in a new superjumbo.

- **Level 4** is true ambiguity where uncertainties are unknown and unknowable. In fact, it may not even be possible to identify the relevant variables. These can often happen after rare events, even Black Swan events, and normally happen after major technological discontinuities. Examples would be forecasting what would happen to the Russian market in the early 1990s after the Berlin Wall came down. Understanding what could result from studying the genome in different species. What could be the demand for renewable energy over next sixty years, which is the time frame that some investments need to consider. As I write this, I am wondering whether Volkswagen, after the emissions crisis, is currently facing Level 4 uncertainty, whereas previously it probably thought it was at Level 1.

Courtney goes on to describe the kinds of strategic decisions that could be impacted by understanding these different levels.

Generic high-risk and low-risk strategic choices

Choice One is Shape or Adapt. This is about the extent to which an organization should seek to lead change in its market, or remain flexible to adapt to whatever may come along. The Shape strategy has a clearly more risk-taking flavour than the 'Adapt' strategy. McKinsey research shows that organizations can be successful in both modes, but also showed that 86 per cent of the most successful businesses were shapers. At the same time, a lot of the least successful businesses were also shapers. So according to our variability definition of risk, this confirms Shape strategies as the higher risk.

As regards Choice One, what impact does the level of uncertainty have on the strategy? Interestingly, while I would expect a fairly linear relationship – something like 'lower levels of uncertainty are better for shaping', according to Courtney – it is not as clear-cut as that. He does suggest that in Level 1 situations, shapers can create an advantage over competition by disrupting the status quo. This looks a lot like Blue Ocean (Kim & Mauborgne, 2005) strategy thinking, where redefining the customer proposition takes the competition out of the equation.

However, he suggests that for both Level 2 and Level 3 situations, adapters are probably better placed. Those whose strategies are to create flexible organizational capabilities, partly through 'buying' more than 'making', can respond better to discrete market changes, or changes within a range. By contrast, the high uncertainty of Level 4 again becomes the domain of the shaper, to create some certainty out of the uncertainty.

He also talks about two other kinds of generic strategic options: Choice Two – Now or Later, generally referring to investment, and Choice Three – Focus or Diversify. These have similarities with the first set, and in each case the first of the two options is the more risk-taking option. And the patterns of when the risk-taking option might make more sense, and when the risk-avoiding option might are also similar.

And in each case, what is clear is that a number of other factors come to play in each case. So, for example, whether or not to Shape or Invest now or Focus – that is, take the high risk route in a Level 1 situation – probably depends on whether or not you have anything worth investing in and that is likely to succeed in shaping the market.

Elephants can feel quite good about this approach because whatever option seems right, we mitigate risk by being better informed. Tigers, on the other hand, may feel there are other things to take into account. We may have a breakthrough idea that should work whatever the level of uncertainty. It may be an inherent character attribute of the organization that makes it clear we can or cannot adopt that strategy. There may be a fundamental principle at stake, or something central to the organization's mission. All of this is covered later in the book.

Scenario analysis

Scenario analysis, described as part of our formal risk management process, is the way in which elephants seek to understand the key variables, and what their impact could be. Scenarios can vary from highly analytical to highly pictorial descriptions of possible futures. I believe the more colourful the scenario, the more useful it can be as the real value is in supporting conversations about the future, and the risks associated with different decisions today. Ensuring that conversations about risk form part of the character of the organization is something I explore more in Chapter 12.

Game theory, as described in Chapter 7 (Section 'Game theory and collaboration'), is a specific example, dealing with one of the most significant variables – what the other party (competition/enemy) might do. One of the origins of game theory was chess, and most chess players can identify with the idea that prior to making a decision, players look ahead several moves to what the opponent might do and what they might do in response. How we play chess is a great example of scenario analysis as-you-go. The more you do it, the better you get at it, until it becomes almost intuitive. It morphs into muscle memory and our elephant heartland becomes the domain of tigers.

To give a flavour for the sort of facilitation that can be offered to support scenario analysis, I have listed below a description of possible techniques:

1. Scenarios focus on key uncertainties and certainties about the future and use this information to construct pen-pictures in an information-rich way in order to provide vivid descriptions of future worlds ... the relationship between critical uncertainties (as they resolve themselves one way or another) important predetermined trends and the behaviour of actors who have a stake in the particular future (and who will tend to act to preserve or enhance their own interests within that future) are thought through in the process ... (Goodwin & Wright, 2004)
2. Start with an issue of concern (e.g. organizational survival), identify trends and uncertainties that impact on the issue, determine degree of inter-relational impact ... put all positive uncertainties in one scenario and all negative ones in another – add trends to both,

check for coherence/plausibility, add likely actions of individuals or organizations with vested interests ... and add a straight extrapolation of the present as the status quo scenario. Then test a business idea, systematically linking competencies and growth feedback loops ... so that testing of business ideas is like 'wind tunnelling' in the context of testing aeroplanes. (Van der Heijden, 1996)

3.   Where degrees of predictability and uncertainty are acceptable – not usually extreme conditions, identify an issue, list on a post-it anything related to the concern and place on the scenario structuring space (two dimensions: less to more predictable, and less to more impact). Go to bottom right (high impact/low predictability) and try and cluster into interrelated elements, then try to identify a smaller number of underlying 'driving forces' which link the uncertainties at a deeper level. Of those identified, which really would make a difference to the decision maker and the business? For each driving force, try to capture extreme outcomes. Experiment by thinking of combinations of the extremes of one of the driving forces which could link with the extremes of others. From these thought experiments, develop the skeletons of three or four scenarios – and give them catchy names. Inspect post-its for the other three quadrants, and place these into one of the scenarios already created. Check if top left could appear in any of the skeleton scenarios. Develop storyline for scenarios – to help, place elements along a timeline for each scenario. Look for causality between elements – makes storyline more plausible. Check all high impact/low predictability elements are covered. If not, consider more scenarios. Then evaluate business ideas against these scenarios.

These may seem complicated but the main point is that they are just tools to help groups tasked with making strategic decisions to have the right kinds of conversations, and more particularly to develop a shared understanding of what are the key variables to consider, and what therefore might be the best risks to take.

Prototyping

Prototyping can be a form of scenario planning, and is well covered by Michael Schrage in his book *Serious Play* (2000). While they are classically known as test forms of physical new products, they can take on a broader definition, as a simulation of some kind of potential future state – for example, covering key aspects, be they financial or otherwise, of organizational life. They can become wellsprings of knowledge, helping organizations to articulate culture or character in different ways. An example of this is the level of perfection needed in a prototype before it is progressed to the next stage. Organizations that are more risk taking will accept lower levels of perfection, and can have a more dynamic progression in prototyping.

Prototypes help address taboos by making it easier or more obvious to ask the questions that you don't feel comfortable asking. What if the *Titanic* does sink? What if the Chernobyl reactor does start to melt down?

Schrage charts the rapid growth of spreadsheets in the 1980s as a form of simulation, starting with Visicalc and progressing to Lotus and Excel. Spectacular changes in global finance came from the power of spreadsheets to support meaningful conversations around the likelihood and impact of different scenarios. They allowed for the effective integration of risk management and opportunity creation – allowing financial managers to become increasingly opportunistic. Specifically, spreadsheet models allowed planners to become clearer about the assumptions they were making about the future, and led to conversations about competing assumptions. So they facilitated a form of risky conversation which otherwise would probably not have happened. Later in Chapter 12, 'Organizational character', I argue that risky conversations are at the heart of an organization's ability to work well with risk.

Ultimately, 'serious play' is about innovative behaviour. It's about the challenge of converting uncertainty into manageable risks or opportunities. More than that, people play with prototypes to capture the unexpected, and to actively create surprise. Like a child, we play for fun, we play to discover, but we also play to win. And in this way we create a connection between the organization's winning aspiration and its capability to innovate.

Chapter 10

Strategic pioneering: Innovation and change

As well as a winning aspiration and an understanding of the key variables, the right risks are often those based on an opportunity to innovate or a need for change. As we deliberately step into new territory, we know less about that territory, so the variability of possible outcomes is that much bigger, that is, it's more risky. We know that innovation and risk are inextricably linked. Innovation means change and change inevitably feels risky.

Innovation and change are not optional. We may debate the level that is needed, but it is not just needed for progress; it's needed for survival. We operate in a VUCA world: it is Volatile, Uncertain, Complex and Ambiguous. These things make it not only difficult to stand still, but also difficult to know which direction to head off in. At Ashridge, within our Strategy and Innovation practice, we are particularly intrigued by the concept of 'dynamic capabilities' as set out by authors such as David Teece (2011). The capabilities we need involve having good sensors to the winds of change, the ability to make important decisions and commit resource to respond to those changes, and the ability to sustain the change momentum.

More specifically, I believe if we want to understand what's behind effective innovation and positive change, we need to look at character. Leadership is directional and involves movement; it's not static. It's taking people from one place to another place, to a new outcome, to a new way of seeing the world and how it works. This is innovative change, and doing this well is what marks out effective innovators from those who are less successful. And character is at the heart of this process. Jim Collins outlined the attributes of the leaders in most successful businesses that he researched in *Good to Great*. He talked of character attributes such as fortitude, humility and discipline. In Chapter 3, I described a character journey that culminated in the Blonay Profiler: Bold Creative, Empathic and Self-Disciplined. Leaders of innovation change need a blend of all three, which is hard to achieve because of the tensions between the dimensions. Most of all, I believe the Bold Creative dimension is the one that is crucial.

I am calling those who have an extra dollop of the Bold Creative dimension 'strategic pioneers'. They are proactive more than they are responsive, and they are intuitive more than they are analytical. They celebrate difference and diversity more than form and order, and are more likely to be found on their own than in a pack. They are natural risk takers.

When I look at the character profiles of different job roles in businesses, the Bold Creatives (those with a higher Bold Creative score than any other dimension) are marginally the least populated group. The Self-Disciplined tend to be in roles that require a high degree of attention to detail, such as finance and administration. The Empathic tend to be in roles where relationship building is important, such as sales or professional roles. Bold Creatives tend to be in creative roles such as in advertising, or in leadership roles. Strategic pioneers generally need a strong suit on this dimension, but they also need to be attentive to the other two. For example, Napoleon was a bold risk taker, who had particularly strong sense of intuition that informed this boldness. It was also informed by an enormous repertoire of knowledge and attention to detail in areas like historical military decisions and artillery.

Our tigers and elephants were born in a story in our research about innovation. This was the race to a global launch of a new product in the fast-growing computer games market. Elephants were needed to make sure all the right processes were in place, with the appropriate attention to detail, and to ask the difficult questions: 'What if this doesn't work as we expect? What if customers don't like that?' Meanwhile, tigers were cutting corners, firing before aiming and going with their intuition. Somehow the organization managed to hold them together, and a successful launch was the result.

It is interesting that Gerstner's book on the transformation of IBM (2002) is called *Who Says Elephants Can't Dance?* This is the story of IBM's transformation over a decade from the early 1990s, from a computer products company to a business services firm, while Gerstner was CEO. In this case, the elephant metaphor is clearly meant to symbolize a large organization, which typically struggles to change very much because of the inertia of its existing expertise and culture. What helps the elephant to dance, I would argue, is the presence of tigers, and particularly a tiger at the helm of the business. He talks about taking two big bets: one to turn IBM into a fully integrated services business, not just the largest but the most influential; the second was to bet that the market would move away from stand-alone computers to network-based solutions. He talks about it as fraught with risk, and suggests: 'There is no such thing as a toe in the water. When you take the plunge, its full body immersion.' Moving to a sporting analogy, his view was that they decided they were going to play offence.

How did he address the problem of loss aversion? The jargon response for any change process is of course the need to articulate what the 'burning platform' is. This is perhaps an unhappy business metaphor in that it relates to the Piper Alpha disaster in 1988, in which many died as a result of jumping from the burning North Sea oil platform into the sea. When asked why they jumped, the survivors' answer was that the platform was burning and they felt they had more chance of surviving by jumping than staying put. I think many probably use the jargon term now without realizing what the origins are. The point is that for people to take on risky change, they need a problem they are trying to get away from. It's not enough just to have a winning aspiration or something you are trying to gain.

For IBM, it was mainly that their heartland, computing, was being trampled on by very competent competitors, and in particular two very dominant competitors: Microsoft in software, and Intel in computer electronics. These firms dominated two areas of competitive advantage in computing, and were known as the 'Wintel' duopoly. The rest of computing, the PC makers like Dell and Compaq, had become heavily commoditized, and were moving more into IBM's heartland of large servers. IBM was being squeezed and needed somewhere else to go, which meant needing to make radical changes to what it did.

I pick up more on the way Gerstner tackled this from an organizational point of view in the next chapter that deals with organizational character. Suffice to say that a number of the messages in this book were played out in this particular IBM story.

I couldn't have a chapter on innovation without also mentioning the Blue Ocean strategy idea, as promoted by Kim and Mauborgne (2005), and to consider how their thinking and case studies tie in with the risk story. Blue Ocean thinking proposes an alternative to Michael Porter's framing of strategy based on achieving competitive advantage (1980), based on a good understanding of the competitive dynamics of the marketplace. Kim and Mauborgne's proposition is that radical innovation takes the competition out of the equation, at least for a season. At the heart of their proposal is that innovating a product or a service based on a better understanding of what customers really value is the way to achieve this. One example of this is the Accor hotel chain, which redesigned the business hotel offer based on what customers were prepared to pay more for, and eliminating features that added cost but no real customer value. So they emphasized reasonable-sized, comfortable and functional rooms, efficient service for booking and check-out, and a competitive price. They took cost out in terms of large foyers and dining areas, and reduced the use of specialized staffing – staff could multitask by operating reception and the bar. Accor developed hotels for a range of different levels of budget, to capture a range of business priorities – and set a new standard for the business-related hospitality sector. Competitors have tried to mimic the offer, but have never fully caught up with Accor's lead in business budget hotels.

The Blue Ocean approach involves higher risk in the short term than the alternative Red Ocean, which is more of the same. This is because there is more variability of possible outcome, compared to the relative comfort of a slowly declining but familiar business model. But we can mitigate this risk through the Inform strategy – gaining insights about what customers actually value as opposed to what can add cost without value.

In our research, we discovered managers talking about innovation and change as risky, but also acknowledging the risks of not changing. We called this phenomenon 'Risk in change; risk of not changing'.

When it comes to change, we come across our old friend 'loss aversion', which I described in Chapter 7 (Section 'Risk compensation') based on the work of Kahneman and Tversky. We are programmed to be disproportionately concerned about what may go wrong, and what we may lose, compared to what could go right and what we may gain. Perhaps it's because our experience tells us that the downside is typically more likely to happen than the upside. We've been promised great things before, and they haven't materialized. We may have been told 'Be bold and go for it', and ended up with egg on our faces. But if we think of risk as negative, we are focused on the downside before we even start. We are loss averse. We don't want to leave our comfortable territory.

This is the innovator's dilemma as encapsulated by Clayton Christensen (2002). Organizations focus on the dark side of dynamic unfamiliarity, and prefer to stay in the stagnant swamp of familiarity. The story of Kodak is a case in point. They preferred the chemical photographic film market that they knew so well – even though it was treating them badly. This was preferable to venturing wholeheartedly into a new market of digital photography, where of course there was always a risk that they would come badly unstuck, perhaps as an also-ran or late entrant who would struggle to catch up.

The essential point that Christensen makes about innovation is that it is often paradoxically destructive. If you are an incumbent in a market, your own 'new' has the potential to help destroy the 'old'. Being prepared to let go, in part at least, of the old is a fundamental challenge to leadership and organizational character.

I was at Procter & Gamble (P&G) when liquid detergents were introduced. Liquid detergent technology was clearly superior in performance to powdered detergents. Unilever took the lead by introducing a new brand, Wisk, which immediately started to take market share from powdered detergents. The problem was that powdered detergents generated a huge proportion of P&G's profits, so introducing a new superior technology was only going to eat into those profits – referred to rather graphically as cannibalization (i.e. eating your own profits!). Unilever doing it under a new brand name helped mitigate some of that cannibalization, but it slowed the progress as consumers needed to become aware and learn to trust a new brand name that they had never seen before. P&G chose a different approach, and launched Tide Liquid and Ariel Liquid as international brand extensions of their existing market leading detergents, Tide and Ariel. This was maximum cannibalization impact – the new technology eating into its own brand franchise, as existing customers simply switched to the new technology. The brand had also maximum impact as P&G took a leading share in the new liquids sector, building on the existing brand franchises. This was an organization that had the character to innovate destructively – the character was based on taking a significant risk, but believing it was the right risk because it was the right thing to do, to give the best technology available to their existing customers.

A similar idea, initially proposed by Joseph Schumpeter in 1942, is that organizations should embrace creative destruction, which was described as a 'process of industrial mutation that incessantly revolutionises the economic structure from within, incessantly destroying the old one, incessantly creating a new one'. Buytendijk talks about this in the context of massive technology changes: cars replacing horse carriages, music downloads succeeding CDs, or email obsoleting fax (2010).

One of the issues is that standard processes and systems do not allow the innovation team to explore new ways of working. The ROI may be too low, or may take too long. It may not seem very attractive, or the size of the potential market may not seem that high. In many cases, organizations decide to create new organization around the innovation. IBM did this by setting up a new business to develop personal computers.

How financial markets value innovation is a key issue, where innovation can be about cash-generating opportunities that are hard to define at the outset. And how financial analysts see things can affect how managers respond to innovation investment. I touched on this in our exploration of the elephant world in Chapter 5 (Section 'The impact of risk on the value of capital'), and concluded that somewhere in the decision-making process, whether it be the analysts or managers, you need tigers – people prepared to trust a gut feel and stick with it, the type of tigers that promoted a Google or a Twitter in the early days.

Alternatively, businesses introduce new propositions into new geographies as the only effective way of launching in that market. Honda penetrated the US motorcycle market by reinventing its target customer segment as adventure bikes for off-roading, coming against the major players of BMW and Harley Davidson. This was very different from its target audience in its home market.

The common denominator in all these scenarios is that innovation is risky, not only because it is moving into unknown territory where the variability of possible outcomes is that much higher, but also because of the impact destructive innovation has on stakeholders with an interest in the incumbent 'old' business.

Nevertheless, the other common point is that the risk of not innovating is often higher, certainly with the benefit of hindsight. So one question is, how can you mitigate the risk of innovation?

Mitigating risk in innovation

It makes sense to define the risk of innovation again around variability, and to revisit our normal curve as a way of representing this. By definition, our expected new return as a result of innovation is assumed to be higher than our current or non-innovation return. But the range of likely new innovation scenario returns is much higher than that of our current non-innovation returns – higher standard deviation indicates higher risk.

So what if we use our 'inform'-based mitigation strategy and can reduce the likelihood of downside returns by effective research and market testing? The idea is that if testing reveals a lower than threshold level return, we stop further development. Then all of a sudden our range of likely outcomes under the innovation scenario looks quite different. Our broader risky normal curve gets its left hand arm cut off. We stop the possibility of big losses arising from innovation that doesn't generate returns. Then when we examine our high risk innovation versus low risk status quo normal curves as shown in Figure 10.1, we only see upside benefit from our higher risk option. That's the theory at least.

At P&G, this was referred to as 'minimizing the cost of failure'. The idea is that we reduce cost, and therefore the risk of failed innovation, by having regular check points or gates at early stages in the process, which provide opportunities to check out of the innovation process before too much is invested. Our old friend 'loss aversion', and its close cousins 'cognitive inertia' and 'confirmation bias', are

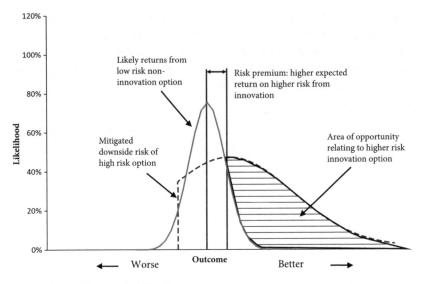

Figure 10.1 Mitigating the risk of innovation

increasingly at work, seeking to trip this process up. At what point is too much invested in the process to feel comfortable to walk away with a guaranteed loss while there is always the chance that it could still be a successful gain? To what extent do we continue to look for reasons why the innovation may not be right, compared to our reasons for persevering?

The Silicon Valley phraseology for this kind of approach is 'failing fast'. The implication is that your expectation is managed because you expect to fail – the thing that's important is that it happens quickly; you learn quickly and move on. Speed is of the essence. It would appear that, not just because in a world where technology is supposedly changing fast and markets are changing swiftly, being ahead of your competition is a distinct advantage. But also, 'failing fast' means you have not got too fond of your pet project; it's not your baby to try and protect. As a result, cognitive inertia doesn't have a chance to set in. And 'failing fast' means you have not built up too much cost before it becomes sunk cost.

It takes a certain type of character (or deep pockets) to be able to walk away from a lot of sunk cost on an innovation project that is going nowhere. I was at Mars Confectionery as a management trainee, in my early career years, when I witnessed our CEO, Forest Mars turn up to our offices in Slough, and tell local management to start ripping up the Banjo line. Banjo was a chocolate wafer bar that was innovative because its main ingredient was a chocolate substitute, which was significantly lower cost than real chocolate. It had tested positively in research and test markets, and gone to full production. The Banjo line was the biggest and most efficient in the factory, using latest technology, for packaging as well as product. However, it was not tracking to plan, and while it was achieving profit, it was not achieving the required level of return on assets that the Mars family set for all its businesses. As far as Mars was concerned, it was therefore taking up valuable space and management time which could be better employed on better ventures. So it was stopped, and the investment written off. This type of risk mitigation is itself high risk for most business leaders.

To recap my proposition, effective strategy and leadership take the right risks, and this means mitigating them effectively, too. Another mechanism behind taking the right types of innovative risks is a concept I have called Creative Juxtaposition.

Creative Juxtaposition

In the early pages of this book, I proposed that an effective risky strategy needed to find a place between the extreme errors of reckless risk taking for its own sake, and cowardly risk avoidance that avoids or postpones the making of tough choices. A strategy needs to be choiceful about risk.

Our research at Ashridge suggested that the optimal approach to risk was a combination of a formal analytical left-brain approach and an informal intuitive right-brain approach, a combination of System 1 and System 2 thinking, because either in isolation was fair game for organizational blind-siding or psychological illusions or traps. Both elephants and tigers are useful – the challenge is taking the right risk.

We understand that a passion for winning creates both an appetite and a need for some risk. But what happens when working in collaboration becomes a more useful paradigm for positive social change than beating competition? How do we bridge the tension between competition and collaboration, and what does it do for our readiness to make risky choices?

When we look at the exploits of apparently successful leaders, we notice a strange dichotomy between risk taking and risk avoidance, an ability to embrace both, keep both in tension, to be able to find those right risks to take and avoid the others. We enquire of those who appear to have risked all to achieve significant victories, and hear that they are preoccupied with avoiding risk wherever possible.

What is happening here?

I believe what is happening is a phenomenon I call Creative Juxtaposition. It's the idea that entities with apparently very different or even opposite polarities come together to bring creative and often positive results. Knowledge that comes from different sources, possibly referring to different subjects, combines to form great ideas – a breakthrough in new knowledge, a great strategy or even a new sense of victory. So much great new positive creative stuff seems to come to us in this way.

The origin of our tigers and elephants story sets the scene for this idea. A fast and effective global launch of an electronic games product was achieved through the combination of methodical elephants and impetuous tigers somehow managing to work together to achieve business victory.

My favourite example of this comes from the world of mathematics – the heartland of formal risk theory. But the example is nothing to do with risk, or at least I have yet to see the connection! It is Pythagoras's theorem, which, if you remember from your school days, stated in rather cryptic fashion: 'The square on the hypotenuse is equal to the sum of the squares on the other two sides'. It was the basis of much mathematical geometry, extended into other trigonometry, and thence into a wide range of practical science applications: wave theory in electrical engineering, or Newtonian physics as applied to mechanical and structural engineering. So quite an important little foundation of knowledge of our world.

When I first learned about it, I remember enjoying working with it but never really appreciated the beauty of it, particularly as it relates initially to three consecutive whole numbers: 3, 4 and 5. Working Pythagoras backwards, you have the idea that if you construct a triangle with sides of length exactly 3 units, 4 units and 5 units, the angle between the shorter sides will be an exact right-angle. The beauty for me is that it should be exact – it's not an approximation, which is rare in interplay between numbers and physical objects. It seems like an extraordinary coincidence of nature – for me, it suggests deliberate design in the heart of our universe. By contrast, the number which defines a perfect circle, Pi, is a long way from being an exact whole number.

So where does Creative Juxtaposition come into this? It's in the discovery of the theorem. Pythagoras was a Greek philosopher and mathematician, who lived around 500 BC. The fact that he specialized in both disciplines already sets the scene for our 'coming together'. We speculate that he learned about triangles and right angles in Egypt, where perfect right angles would have been important, for example, in the construction of the pyramids. It would have been impossible to have constructed them without perfectly right-angled corner stones, as the resulting structure would not have been based on a perfect square as we witness today. He would have learned in particular that something like a papyrus reed folded into 12 exact segments could then be folded into a triangle of sides length 3 notches, 4 notches and 5 notches, and that this would form a perfect right-angle.

Quite separately, he learned of arithmetic from Phoenicia, in which he would have learned about the properties of numbers multiplied by themselves, squares. And the curious idea that the squares of three sequential whole numbers 3, 4 and 5 are related by the equation: 3 squared added to 4 squared are equal in quantity to 5 squared. He would have recalled his lessons on papyrus and pyramid construction, and noted that the numbers representing the sides of his right angled triangle could actually be related arithmetically. Who was it that then, I wonder, asked: 'I wonder if you would find the same numerical relationship of side dimensions in all triangles with right angles'. And through this process of combining different disciplines of knowledge, amazing new knowledge with wide reaching usefulness is born. We have the process of Creative Juxtaposition.

I see this idea of Creative Juxtaposition at the heart of all sorts of different forms of creativity. The atoms of hydrogen gas and oxygen gas combine to form the most unlikely and miraculous of molecules, the water molecule. Animals of different genders combine to create new life. Animal and plant combine in pollenization to create new plant life and food for animals. There's Gilbert & Sullivan, Morecambe & Wise, Flanders & Swan, Marks & Spencer, Procter & Gamble. In Chinese tradition, there is the idea in Yin and Yang, that contrasting concepts, light and dark, sunny and shady, sun and moon, combine to create a whole picture. This book explores a number of yin and yangs that combine to create something bigger than the sum of its parts: risk and strategy, tiger and elephant, danger and opportunity.

Buytendijk picks up on this idea when he talks about working with dilemmas, and combining contracts (2010). He gives examples: Senseo is a one-touch button machine for espresso coffee based on collaboration between Philips and Douwe Egberts: Philips created the appliance; Douwe Egberts a special blend of coffee. Or there is the Nike+ system, a collaboration between Nike and Apple where a Bluetooth sensor that fits in your Nike shoe sends running statistics to your iPod. In fact, part of the innovation gifting of Steve Jobs was to bring ideas from different sources together: artful design and functional technology, extreme secrecy and an open market for applications.

Strategic Intuition

Creative Juxtaposition is the cousin of 'Strategic Intuition', a concept I learned about from a book of that subject by a professor at Columbia University, William Duggan (2007). His idea, in part at least, is that in great strategic breakthroughs, left brain and right brain thinking combine to give birth to new thinking. The closest to the language that I have been using is that tigers and elephants get together. On top of that, you have elephants that are already great at synthesizing different ideas, so you get a kind of double whammy. He takes his examples from the worlds of science, combat, business and religion.

In science, for example, he talks about Thomas Kuhn's 'The Structure of Scientific Revolutions' (Kuhn 1962) in which Kuhn describes how scientific achievement really happens, and explains some of the origins of the scientific method. We see Creative Juxtaposition in the combination of the Greeks and the later work of Copernicus and Newton. Newton says as much that he could never have come up with his own breakthroughs in thinking, contributing to massive engineering innovation, without drawing from the ideas of those who came before. He writes: 'If I have seen farther, it is by standing on the shoulders of giants.' Kuhn develops this idea of scientists standing in a bend in the road, looking backwards to where they have come from, and forwards to where they are going, and it's in this place that the new thinking occurs.

When Duggan turns then to examples of Strategic Intuition in combat, he draws on the strategic work of von Clausewitz, who had in turn been heavily influenced by the achievements of one Napoleon Bonaparte. Von Clausewitz in his book on strategy *On War*, describes the concept of 'Coup d'oeil' as the key to strategy, in explaining the success of Napoleon. He sets out to explain the flashes of insight for which Napoleon was known throughout his life, using this concept. He is able to combine different key pieces of information: his knowledge of artillery and what it is capable of; his understanding of recent battle encounters with the British fleet; and his knowledge of the geography around Toulon. These lead to an insight in which he predicts that when artillery will achieve a position on a certain hill, the English fleet will leave. The rest is history – his victory at Toulon propelled Napoleon to high position in France, and was the first of many famous victories.

Duggan then lists examples of Strategic Intuition in the business world. Steve Jobs combines the inventions of his Silicon Valley colleagues with understanding of great design, with understanding of market economics – and the Apple Mac is born. Bill Gates and Paul Allen combine the knowledge of machine programming code with the appearance of the new small computer, the Altair. And so software programmed into microcomputers arrives – and a big player, IBM, is looking for a partner to help tap into the micro market. His resolution in pursuing that opportunity was the pivotal moment for the success of Microsoft.

These leaders in science, combat and business all are able to take the right risks, leading to big steps forward in their particular fields. Those right risks come from both an analytical elephant approach, and an intuitive tiger approach. The appropriate analysis together with the insight leads both to the breakthrough and the resolve to take the risk to make it real.

I believe there is another key ingredient that paves the way for this Creative Juxtaposition to happen at all; one phrase for it is Intelligent Ignorance.

Intelligent Ignorance

I believe at the heart of effective innovation is a concept that I love the sound of: Intelligent Ignorance. This is connected to a phenomenon I have increasingly become aware of in the work we do at Ashridge, and particularly in my executive coaching. This idea is that the question is worth more than the answer. Very simply, I suppose, the recognition or acceptance that we don't know leads us to want to find out more, and it is this process that really leads to breakthrough insights.

Stuart Firestein gave a TED talk in 2012, and has written a book *Ignorance: How It Drives Science* (2012), which sets out the case for Intelligent Ignorance. His favourite proverb appears to be: 'It is difficult to find a black cat in a dark room, especially when there is no cat'. He tells us that while science is taught in schools and textbooks as what we know, this distorts the real world of science. Scientists generally spend most of their lives with what we don't know. It is indeed more about questions than answers. There is the lament that the more we know, the more we know that we don't know. He quotes two great scientists: (a) Marie Curie, who said after obtaining her second graduate degree: 'One never notices what has been done; only what remains to be done' and (b) James Clerk Maxwell, who said: 'Thoroughly conscious ignorance is the prelude to every real advance in science'.

The challenge with this, however, is that we still need to make decisions and take risks, even though we don't know. The irony is that the mindset of Intelligent Ignorance that got us to the breakthrough insight is the enemy of the mindset that would now take a risky decision. So it is a relatively rare skill to be able to hold both in tension: the 'not knowing' and the 'decision to act'.

Commerce and public management are the pragmatic ends of science. Good science, as Firestein argues, needs to celebrate and work with ignorance, as this is the basis for new science and ultimately for innovation. Pure science doesn't need to make premature decisions about truth, nor about the application of that truth. It only needs to make decisions about methods for working with ignorance. Firestein talks about Faraday, whose amazing discoveries about electricity have led to a very different world. But he had no idea what electricity might be good for. When asked about possible uses of electromagnetic fields, he responded: 'Of what use is a newborn baby?'

Another example Firestein gives us is the PET scanner; PET stands for Positron Emission Tomography. It is used in hospitals, often combined with other scanners, to give a more complete picture of the internal workings of the body. It is particularly used in diagnosing cancer and the progress of cancer treatment. In 1928, the physicist Paul Dirac was investigating electrons in quantum mechanical terms, and proposed there must be an anti-electron, a positron, to fit with a proposed quantum mechanics equation. But no one had ever observed a positron until an experiment by another physicist, Carl Andersen, using new technology called cloud chambers, discovered the existence of positrons. Neither Dirac nor Andersen had any idea of an application for this discovery; it was just work in aid of discovering more about the unknown. Forty years later, the knowledge about the positron was used in developing an important new piece of medical technology. Actually, we witnessed another example of Creative Juxtaposition, as the science of positrons was combined with knowledge of new tomographic imaging techniques and advances in computer technology.

At the pragmatic end of the spectrum, the crunch comes when a decision is needed to commit significant resources to the unknown. It's as if what is needed is an amazing cocktail of discipline in synthesizing what is known, humility in accepting a level of ignorance, and the bold-ness to act regardless. This sounds remarkably like Jim Collins's recipe for effective business leadership in *Good to Great* (2001) – the combina-tion of humility, discipline and resolve. These resonate with the charac-ter attributes that we investigate with the Blonay Character Profiler: Bold Creative, Empathic and Self-Disciplined.

All of this links with the idea of creative failure, and the Silicon Valley 'fail fast' mindset that I referred to in Chapter 6 on tigers. Matthew Syed in his book *Black Box Thinking* (2015) makes the case for why fail-ure is essential to success and to creative breakthroughs. He outlines the process of interrogating errors as an integral part of a strategy for success – and he contrasts the different approach of the aviation indus-try and healthcare. The former rigorously declare and examine mistakes – including near mistakes – in order to reduce aviation accidents with incredible statistics to back up how aviation safety has improved over the last few decades. Sadly there is no such culture in healthcare, and there has sadly been no such reduction in deaths through healthcare mistakes over the decades. There is clearly something different in the character of both types of organization – a factor I will explore more in Chapter 12 dealing with organizational character.

The Creative Juxtaposition of pulling together what we do know to address what is not known, the intuition that combines and believes we have something worth deciding on, and the resolve then to act on that and see it through are the marks of Duggan's *Strategic Intuition* (2007), and von Clausewitz' *Coup D'oeil* (1976). It is the point where tiger and elephant meet.

Innovation often needs that breakthrough moment, followed by the resolve to see it through. In a sense, a breakthrough is a Black Swan: no one really expects it to happen. Just as you are thinking, 'Oh no, here we go, just a load more white swans', up pops a black one! You have a 'Eureka' moment in the bath, or the gravity apple lands on your head. So the point about Black Swans is that they can be good things. They can also be very bad things. In both counts, what's both glorious and frustrating about them is that they are hard to plan for.

Chapter 11

Working with the Black Swan: Reputation and crisis

In Chapter 7, when we considered the mind games that can influence our approach to risk, we talked about Taleb's Black Swan. While he described these as highly improbable events, they are also paradigm-busters in the same sense as radical innovation is a paradigm-buster: they bring about a big change in how we see things. The difference is that they tend to happen without deliberate or intended human intervention; what is considered normal today, based on our experience up to now, may not be normal in the future. 'All swans are white' is no longer a valid belief, once we discover a black swan.

As we have considered risk up to now, we have tended to think of limited ranges of different types variability in the future – some more predictable than others. But for many, risk is about working with the extremes of variability – thinking about unlikely outcomes which could have significant impact. As we have discussed, these tend to be high on the agenda in public management, which carries a primary remit of protecting citizens against extremes of danger. It is also falling increasingly on the agenda of business, where corporate crises are becoming a more regular feature of media reports.

The question is, for a book like this about strategy, can or should strategy address the possibility of these extreme outcomes, and if so, how? I believe the key here is the relationship that strategy has with organizational character, and the extent to which one influences the other. So I shall explore what aspects of organizational character can help organizations work more effectively with Black Swan events; and I do that in the next chapter. Before I do that, I want to unpack why this is an important aspect of risk.

Certainly, when I look at the types of risk that leaders are primarily concerned with, reputational risk, and ways of either avoiding or handling crises effectively, is generally very high on the list of priorities.

In the public sector, reputation impacts votes and is therefore critical to the ability to retain roles of leadership. In the private sector, reputation impacts brand image, customer behaviour, sales, profits and ultimately also the ability to retain roles of leadership.

An increasing proportion of the market value of businesses is made up of brand value, compared to physical assets. Fifty-three per cent of the value of Fortune 500 companies is accounted for through intangible assets – estimated at a global value of US$24 trillion. Interbrand and Citibank in 1998 found the total value of FTSE 100 companies was £842bn, with goodwill accounting for 71 per cent. In contrast, ten years ago, goodwill accounted for 44 per cent of the total. A separate Interbrand study estimated that 25 per cent of the world's total financial wealth is tied up in intangible assets (CEB, 2015).

So how damaging can a reputation crisis be? When BP experienced its catastrophic oil rig failure in the Gulf of Mexico, its share price plummeted to less than half its value prior to the crisis. This represented over £50 billion of reduced market value, well in excess of any likely damages that would accrue from the disaster. What was the reason for this extreme reaction? Almost undoubtedly the impact on the reputation of the BP brand name. One of the problems with oil companies that have vertically integrated businesses is that the brand is emblazoned on very public service stations. And in a competitive market, customers do make choices based on brand reputation.

As I write, the full extent of the 'cheating software' crisis at Volkswagen is still unravelling. When it became public knowledge, Volkswagen's share price dropped nearly 50 per cent. This represents significantly more than the cost of recovering the implicated vehicles, and even that of reimbursing customers for their costs in fixing the problem. It reflects the lost value of the brand. People bought Volkswagen cars, often at a premium price compared to other similar vehicles, because of what the brand represented, in terms of quality and performance you can trust. Much of that value has been eroded by the recent crisis.

The government has recently passed the Modern Slavery Act, which has raised the issue of possible human rights abuses in the global supply chain of many of the UK's major businesses. Ashridge have teamed up with the Ethical Trading Initiative (ETI), a charity helping businesses to collaborate in addressing ethical trade issues. Together we are conducting research into how ETI's members, many of whom are leading retailers, are addressing these issues.

One thing is clear: ethical trade, global human rights issues and now specifically the possibility of slavery or forced labour in the supply chain are becoming more common agenda items in the board meetings of these companies. Our research highlights a number of factors that are driving this interest, ranging from the organization's core values and concern about the health of workers to the legislation itself. Our research showed that the single biggest factor driving the need for change is reputational risk.

We tried to understand how reputational risk can manifest in doing harm to the business. It is clearly not just the fact that customers could react to a bad story by boycotting the retailer concerned. In fact, the people we spoke to were dubious as to the extent that this would happen. It was also employees who were concerned about these things. And investors are increasingly showing an interest. And at the heart of it is the growing reach and power of media – social media in particular – which has little or no authoritative controls.

So this category of risk raises additional questions. Would we work with reputational risk any differently from other types of risk in terms of thinking about strategy? Do tigers and elephants have a different take on how to handle it? How does it impact our sense of a winning aspiration? What illusions and traps do we need to watch out for?

The BP example indicates fairly clearly that reputational risk is a strategic issue. Wiping off more than half your market capitalization suggests it's strategic – enough for the Chairman Lord Browne to resign. In the public sector, arguably there is no type of risk that could be more strategic.

So what is the best way of handling it? Is this one for elephants or tigers? There clearly is a role for elephants. The impact of reputational failures can clearly be measured, as in the case of BP. And clearly there can be a whole raft of formal improvements put in place to significantly reduce the likelihood of a recurrence of such a crisis. And this could be evaluated using cost/benefit analysis, which could be assessed by any number of board reporting teams and committees. All of this is good elephant activity, mitigating risk through better information, and sharing the decision across swathes of management in governance roles.

So is there a role for tigers when working with this kind of risk? It would certainly appear that it is all about danger and very little opportunity. That is until you consider the full implications of formal reputational risk management.

The clearest way to avoid reputational risk is not to have a reputation at all. For a public service, this would mean not to become a public leader, or not to go into politics at all. For BP, this could mean a withdrawal from retailing, to remove the brand from the public domain. It could mean to stop drilling for oil. Clearly, society would be the loser if this approach to reputational risk were to be widely adopted.

And this is becoming an issue in the health sector. Health is understandably a hot topic in terms of public interest, and therefore a key focus for media attention. Hospitals are regularly being exposed either for poor health performance, poor service or poor financial management. As a result of this reputational risk (along with all kinds of other risks), hospital chief executives are increasingly finding their jobs on the line. One of the ways in which individuals manage the reputational risk of being an exposed and possibly deposed chief executive is not to apply for the role in the first place. Consequently, it is becoming increasingly difficult to find effective and much-needed candidates to run our hospitals. So this form of risk reputation management is clearly not serving the public interest.

From a tiger perspective, there must be a role for a less formal, more intuitive approach to personal reputational risk management in the health sector. This is an approach that recognizes the opportunities as well as the dangers in the role of running a hospital.

The key thing about tigers is that they work quickly. Often the single biggest need in working with risk in a crisis is to be able to respond quickly. But this in turn brings its own risks.

Working with risk in crisis

There is clearly a difference between how we prepare for the possibility of crisis, and how we cope with one, once we are in it. In my experience, risk management texts around the subject of crisis tend to confuse the two. There are similarities, but first of all, what are the differences?

Preparing is more akin to strategic risk, whereas dealing with the crisis is different. As this book is about risk in strategy, dealing with risk in crisis is somewhat outside the scope of what I am covering. However, there are probably aspects of crisis management, as it has come to be referred to, that are useful when we think of risk in strategy making. Let's consider some of the other differences.

The biggest difference is time; specifically, the timeliness of making tough decisions. In a strategic context, this is generally not critical; clearly in a crisis it is. In fact, most of the lessons that distinguish well managed crises from those that were less well managed are around how fast decisions were made. And in the heart of this is a dilemma that we can relate to our strategic decision making: in the fog of a crisis, good information about what has happened may be slow to emerge, so there is more uncertainty surrounding a fast decision compared to a slower more considered one, in which time we might hope to have better information. At the same time, delay can have significantly more negative consequences than fast action. Again, we have a 'risk if you do, risk if you don't' situation. In this sense, it is no different to our strategic decision making.

As we know, fast decision making is tiger territory. In the absence of better information, we may need to look more to intuition. A number of factors may help inform that intuition, but there is a point where the leader senses 'this is the right thing to do now'. Sometimes, with hindsight, they get it right; at other times they don't. Let's look at a case study of two comparable crises, one which appeared to be well handled in retrospect, and the other, not so well. I am thinking of the cases of Tylenol and Perrier (Regester & Larkin, 2005), both consumer brands that experienced serious contamination crises.

Tylenol, Perrier and other crises

Johnson & Johnson (J&J), a US consumer goods and pharmaceutical company, has a market leading painkiller product called Tylenol. In September 1982, J&J became aware that cyanide-laced Tylenol tablets had caused three deaths in the Chicago area. Immediately, they made decisions and took action. They looked at the worst possible scenario in the case of the health of customers. As a result, they lost no time in recalling millions of bottles, and spent half a million dollars communicating to doctors. As news spread, as many as 250 potential deaths were associated with it. J&J tested 8mn tablets and found 75 contaminated tablets, all from one batch linked to the Chicago area. The final death toll was seven, all of them in Chicago, but alarm had already spread throughout the USA. Surveys showed that 94 per cent of consumers were aware of the problem. Its next action was to be the first pharmaceutical company to introduce tamper-resistant packaging. It took its time in reintroducing Tylenol to the market. Within five months, it had recovered 70 per cent of the one-third share of the huge market it previously had, and to this day has recovered 100 per cent of its lost market share. It won a Public Relations award. It had clearly positioned itself as consumer champion, gave meaning to corporate social responsibility (CSR), and demonstrated high communication expertise. However, they never found the person responsible for contaminating the drug and effectively murdering seven people.

The key was imagining the worst and acting fast, even though J&J didn't know how extensive the tampering had been. It could have restricted itself to the Chicago area, where the only known incidents had occurred and saved millions of dollars in the cost of the recall, and limited the exposure of the bad news. It came clean about the problem, took swift steps to consider further preventative action and invested quickly in those processes. Had it not done this, it almost definitely would not have recovered its position.

The story of Perrier is a little different. In 1990, a laboratory in North Carolina found traces of Benzene in samples of Perrier's mineral water. The company's approach was to dismiss this as a 'little affair which in a few days, will all be forgotten'. Twenty-four hours later, its share price was falling like '10 green bottles'. In the USA, the company decided to clear bottles off its shelves, but the French company put this down to American wimpishness. By the time they did respond, with withdrawals, the damage to the reputation was done. MORI research showed Perrier's identity to have been the second most damaged as a result of corporate error. It might have done better, but when eventually it returned to the shelves, supported by a 'Perrier is back' campaign, it had smaller 750 ml bottles at the same price as the 1L bottles were before the crisis. The idea that customers should pay for the mistake did not go down very well.

The Brent Spar crisis (Regester & Larkin, 2005) is another interesting example of a failure in reputation management, which was about misunderstanding of public opinion and the role of the media. In 1995, Shell UK was faced with decommissioning the redundant Brent Spar North Sea oil platform. They had planned to tow it out to the Atlantic Ocean, and then to sink it. They had researched this, and calculated that it was the best environmental solution. However, they ended up having to dismantle it on land – the second best environmental option, due to a very effective pressure group. It became an international crisis involving German and UK governments. In a BBC Newsnight interview with Jeremy Paxman, having just announced plans to abandon deep water disposal, the Shell representative responded: 'Am I expected to react every day to the misinformation that the media takes in ...?' Needless to say, this didn't help his cause. The incident was an example of a failure to manage the real issue: public opinion. The case suffered from poor communication, failure to explain scientific information clearly and succinctly, poor intelligence on Greenpeace and generally a lack of consistency of response.

Since then, the influence of the media has increased considerably, particularly with the growth of social media. Special interest groups seek opportunities to 'sound the alarm', which at some point elicit a data-based response from industry. This can become a game of reputation tennis, with the excitement growing with each strike of the ball. The public can become anxious and start to avoid the brand(s) in questions, sales decline and the temperature starts to soar up, with more reputational energy exerted by industry in a bid to minimize the damage. Eventually a more balanced view emerges, sometimes involving government and legislation, and the activists move on.

One of the lessons from these cases is that organizations facing crisis need the ability to envision worst case scenarios, particularly where that concerns the health of the public. They also need to be able to make fast decisions, even where the financial risks are high. Clearly, this requires a more intuitive approach to decision making, where comprehensive facts will not be readily available but there will still be some important facts to take into account: how many incidents so far, what is possible health hazard, or what is the likely cost of product recall? The combination of selective use of information, openness to all scenarios and intuition seems to be the winning formula. We have perhaps a similar process to our von Clausewitz *coup d'oeil*, Strategic Intuition – the ability to mix key facts with intuition and the boldness then to make a tough decision. In other words, the ability to bring elephants and tigers together.

Although these cases appear exceptional, there are many of them. Business schools seek increasingly to draw on case studies of crises to help managers to develop their capabilities to respond in these situations. In recent years, it would appear an increasing proportion of these crises have been triggered by ethical failures in leadership. Theodore Malloch's book *The End of Ethics… and a Way Back* (Malloch 2013) charts a long list from the financial industry alone, cases including Lehman Brothers, Bear Stearns, the Ratings Agencies, LIBOR fixing, MF Global, Tyco, Bernie Madoff's Ponzi Scheme and Worldcom, and concludes that this appears to be a serial problem that still has not been fixed way beyond the initial troubles of the banking crisis. I have mentioned others already in this book, which are apparently the result of failures in ethical leadership: BP and Volkswagen, for example. And the question remains: how do you plan for them? To what extent, can leaders be proactive?

My Ashridge colleague Eve Poole talks about the need for organizations to develop 'canaries in the mine', developing early warning approaches to spot trouble ahead. All of this points to a fundamental need for organizations to be able to be more alert to these kinds of reputational risks, while also to be able to take the right risks that move the organization forward.

Chapter 12

Organizational character

Strategy for an organization needs to be based on understanding the organization. Some say you start with the organization and work back towards the strategy – sometimes referred to as the Resource-Based View, based on work done by Wernefelt (1984). Others suggest you start with the external environment and customers or stakeholders to develop strategy, and then calculate the implications for organizational capabilities, to be able to deliver that strategy. And tension holders like me, of course, suggest that it's actually a bit of both.

We support the idea that organizations need to develop 'dynamic capabilities' as proposed by Teece (2011), in order to respond more effectively to a business market and environment that appear to be increasingly Volatile, Uncertain, Complex and Ambiguous (VUCA), in other words, the ability to sense the environment, to seize the initiative by committing the right resources and the ability to sustain the changes by transforming the organization. My Ashridge colleague James Moncrieff has proposed that the correct organizational response to a VUCA world is itself VUCA, which, in this case, would stand for Velocity, Ubiquity, Connectivity and Agility.

When I think about strategy and risk, all this discussion helps but I think we are looking for something more distinctive in the nature of the organization. It's more edgy and more specific than just talking about organizational culture; I believe it's one part of that culture. I call it the character of the organization. And it's in the make-up of the character that we find that appetite for and attitude towards risk.

Business school colleagues who have done a lot of work on the impacts of mergers and acquisitions tell me that the toughest aspect to handle is the merging of two different cultures, but actually more specific than that, the merging of one organizational culture that sits comfortably with risk taking with another that doesn't.

When I consider the topics of the last two chapters, effective innovation and working with the crisis and reputation, while they seem quite different, I believe there are organizational character attributes which help with both, in creating organizational character that works well with risk. I believe that we are discovering that some of those attributes are:

• Accepting and working with the imperfect
• Accepting and working with ignorance
• Accepting failure but failing fast
• Reconciling innovation with destruction
• Countering the illusion of risk management as a specialist activity; we are all in the risk game; variability is our job calling
• Countering the illusion of confirmation bias and asking what would I look for if my beliefs or assumptions were wrong?
• Selecting the right variables to understand better – not being paralysed with analysis
• Looking for the 'A-ha' moments when different ideas collide
• Working with intuition

In our modern slavery research, one of the regular factors that our respondents referred to as driving action to address the problem was Corporate DNA. This for me is another way of describing organizational character, except for the implication that Corporate DNA has been there from the outset, whereas character can probably be developed or will change over time. What is also interesting is that this DNA was expressed in different ways, even though the resulting behaviour was similar. The whole point of DNA is that each one is different. It's what makes all of us so diverse, each with different gifts, talents, etc.

DNA is often woven into the character of the organization. Procter & Gamble (P&G) established principles when the company was formed which were largely passed on through generations of CEOs. These were sustained through an organizational system that primarily promoted managers from within its own ranks. This meant that P&G chief executives and senior managers had worked their way up through the ranks of the organization, and become trained in both competence and culture. Publications such as *Eyes on Tomorrow* (Schisgall, 1981), which described the history of Procter and Gamble, were made available to all staff. While I was there, a leaflet written by the chairman, Owen Butler, entitled *The Special Qualities of P&G People*, was issued to all staff. These described P&G DNA. The latter started with a quote by James Gamble: 'When you cannot make pure goods and full weight, go to something else that is honest, even if it is breaking stone.' This set out the importance of integrity within the organization.

It also set out what P&G called the Spirit of Exploration. It is described more fully as: 'Nothing ... is as good as it can be or as good as it ought to be. Just doing better than others is not good enough. We must also know more and do better today than we did yesterday, and do better tomorrow than we do today.' Butler talks about these qualities as the character of the organization. And the Spirit of Exploration is the spirit of the pioneer. P&G promoted strategic pioneering as core to its character.

Some organizations deliberately set out to change their character. Under Gerstner during the 1990s, IBM moved from primarily a product manufacturer to a leading business services firm, and the most difficult part of this was changing the culture, the character even, of the organization. One interesting example of this was his approach to a specific corporate value: 'respect for the individual'. This sounds like a laudable value, but in IBM's case it had migrated to one of 'entitlement'. Managers believed that they could do their thing and should be respected for it. The problem was that IBM needed to change what 'their thing' was in order to survive and thrive in the new market. This required risk from the top to tackle and change this core element in the culture of the organization.

Another aspect of the IBM organization that Gerstner tackled was the contradictions between stated strategic priorities and behaviours that were actually rewarded. Examples were having teamwork as a stated value, but rewarding individual performance at the expense of collaboration. Another was having responsiveness to customers as a core value, but only allowing the finance department to authorize pricing changes, seeing quality as the top priority but seeking to cut the cost of activities that enhance quality. These types of inconsistencies are symptomatic of organizational leadership that fails to make the tough choices. Referring again to Treacy and Wiersema's disciplines (1995), where an organization fails to identify and prioritize a core discipline, it is likely to retain such inconsistencies. It would seem that Gerstner was prioritizing a Customer Intimacy discipline, but this had implications not just for what IBM needed to do more of, but also what it needed to stop. No wonder he saw the challenge as taking risks and making big bets. The change he was leading was radical and therefore risky. In his words, it was akin to 'preparing a tame lion for the jungle'. This was not dipping a toe in the water of change, this was full body immersion.

As I started to describe in Chapter 3, making tough choices for a preferred organizational discipline had implications for the character of the organization. In the case of P&G, it was there in the DNA of the organization from the outset, and needed processes to preserve and build on it. In the case of IBM, it needed to change. In either event, and in the case of any organization, it is likely to be different.

Revisiting the character profiler

To recap, the story I told in Chapter 3 was of the development of the Blonay Character Profiler. It came out of the strategy work I was doing with Treacy & Wiersema's model of organizational disciplines for market leadership: Product Leadership, Customer Intimacy and Operational Excellence. I found myself regularly asking the question: what type of leaders and staff does an organization need that seeks to excel in one of these disciplines? So I came up with a personal profile model that mimicked these disciplines, based on the character attributes of Bold Creative, Empathic and Self-Disciplined.

I have found that individual character profiles tend to follow job roles more closely than they do specific organizations. So, for example, finance people more often have a tendency towards a stronger Self-Disciplined score, while those in professional roles like consultants tend to have a stronger Empathic score. Senior managers are the group most likely to have strong Bold Creative scores, but within the senior manager group, there is generally a mix of profiles.

I did, however, suggest that the profiler could provide a model for organizational character. My place of work, Ashridge, appears to have a tendency towards the Empathic attribute amongst a sample of staff. I suspect this would be higher than is the case for other business schools. This may be because organization consultants make up a significant proportion of the faculty. It may be because we focus on developing leaders, and are particularly interested in the behavioural sciences aspect of leadership, more so than some of the more technical aspects of management (finance, marketing, operations, systems, etc.). What it means for our appetite for risk in strategic decision making is that we employ more of an elephant approach, and mitigate risk by sharing and consulting. It means some decisions have taken longer to make; it means, I believe, that other tough choices are not made at all. It's part of the way our organizational character impacts our approach to risk in strategic decisions.

A number of the pointers emerging from the Ashridge research on risk (West et al., 2014) had implications for organizational character. We noted that principles and values often impacted the way in which decisions are made with regard to risk. We noted that accountability for risk across the organization needed particular care. We noted that in order to handle risk well, organizations need to encourage conversations about risk, even if those conversations are risky in themselves. I want to develop each of these in turn.

If risk-taking decisions are often based on personal values and principles, then understanding how those manifest themselves across the organization must be important. The Character Profiler teases out how these might be in tension. The Self-Disciplined and the Empathic are a case in point. For example, the Self-Disciplined might prioritize efficiency, financial performance and numerical measures, while the Empathic would prioritize relationship and the welfare of people. The Self-Disciplined would value integrity and justice, and be more of a meritocracy, while being more ready to be harsh but fair. The Empathic would value care and mercy, while needing to live with more blurred boundaries, and less transparency of information. In caricature almost, we paint a picture of two very different types of organization.

And these two organizational character types have different implications for how they would handle risk. Both have a primarily elephant approach to risk, but the Self-Disciplined seek to mitigate risk by being better informed, while the Empathic seek to mitigate risk by sharing, involving others, consulting and collaborating.

Bold Creative organizations, on the other hand, value courage and creativity. And this can be at the expense of both relationship and numerical rigour. Bold Creatives value inspired thinking and straight talking. Consensus, or concern for the feelings of others, is not a core part of the culture. Nor is perfection in analysis and thinking; they may even celebrate imperfection, and may be awash with stories of colourful failures. These are tiger-like organizations. They like to move fast – they look dangerous to any organization with which they might compete with. They are often run by Bold Creative leaders in quite a despotic style – or they are populated extensively by Bold Creative tigers. If it's the latter, they probably mostly appear quite chaotic. Most importantly, they embrace risk.

Does this description make you think of any organizations you may recognize? My sense is that there are a smattering of these in Silicon Valley, but I would love to know what anyone based there thinks of my suppositions. Can relationships really thrive in these tiger-like organizations, or do they always fall on shaky ground? Does anyone find it easy to do anything thoroughly? Does sound analysis count for very much?

Whichever type of organizational character prevails, all have to deal with some degree of uncertainty. As we have seen from the crises we explored in the previous chapter, danger lurks somewhere in the background, whether you go looking for it or not. Organizations strive in different ways to make themselves more robust. While the theory that 'all swans are white' holds sway, this can work; it's when the black swan comes along that they can struggle.

Taleb, author of the *Black Swan*, had an answer for this, which he called anti-fragility.

Anti-fragility

Taleb's thesis (2012) is that in the face of uncertainty with potentially negative consequences, organizations experience what he calls 'fragility', and compensate for this by developing 'robustness' in finding ways to reduce uncertainty – health and safety measures, bureaucratic governance procedures or sophisticated models equivalent to what we term 'formal risk'. His view is that this doesn't work well because it fails to recognize that uncertainty is fundamental to the nature of things, and has its own mechanisms for compensating for itself. He argues that we need to find ways of using uncertainty to our advantage – developing the idea of maximizing upside potential by changing the odds – developing what he calls anti-fragility. We need to develop systems that correct themselves to generate improvement, even when things do go wrong, which he says is really only a reflection of the natural world.

Our bodies work in anti-fragile ways. While our minds typically enable us to work appropriately with risk, they generally do not seek to avoid it altogether. We will still cross a road, while we may choose not to try to cross a busy multi-lane road. We will still engage in different kinds of sport which can lead to injury, although there may come a time when, as footballers with some coaxing from our wives, as in my case, we decide it is probably time to hang up our boots. We visit countries that experience contagious disease, but we take precautions through the use of vaccinations.

When we do experience injury or become exposed to infection, our bodies have amazing mechanisms for recovering the situation. Armies of white blood cells immediately get called to the infected area, and work in harmony together to attack any invading infection cells. The infection is often contained and only manages to make limited progress in its body invasion plans. Our skin is wonderfully effective at containing life-giving blood and keeping friendly cells in, and unfriendly cells out. But its important flexibility and sensitivity means it can be cut open. Then blood around the cut, as soon as it is exposed to outside air, is conditioned to start to solidify to a sticky coagulant, which in minutes can start to form a seal to replace the skin. And it is then the fertile 'soil' on which new skin can start to grow, and connect up with the existing skin, ultimately achieving an amazing recovery. With smaller cuts, the recovery is so complete that there is no evidence of the history of the cut ever having been there. That's anti-fragility! No wonder we are happy to have a go at a risky sport, or cross a road when we need to.

Plants are even more anti-fragile! In fact, they promote risk as a means of making their presence felt. Flowers with seeds and nectar invite attack from marauding flying insects, so that the seeds can then die and be buried – just so that new life can emerge from underground. Pruning may kill the branch, but just invites more vigorous growth from the remaining stump.

What can we learn for human organizations from these natural anti-fragile experiences? First, risk is literally part of the lifeblood of the system. Without seeds dying and being buried, we would all starve. White blood cells make up about 1 per cent of blood, and their primary job is working with risk. Secondly, proactive and responsive processes are both valid, and work with each other. Mitigation and contingency are part of a coherent system. Our brains help us decide when to risk – our automatic physiological processes are designed to mop up where the variables actually exceed the brains assessment. As in emerging automotive technology, we need both active and passive safety systems.

And the other thing I notice is that the different anti-fragile elements all work together to deal with the risk. Each part knows its part, and plays it with the same aim – whether that be prevention or recovery. The brain helps the body to avoid dangerous situations, and the body responds. The brain remains effective because the red blood cells keep feeding it. Once there is an invasion, it is the white not the red cells that are called into action to deal with it – as a combined coherent force. And meanwhile the coagulants in the blood perform their own distinctive role in sealing up the wound, not undermining the efforts of the white cells to attack, or the red cells to continue feeding the source of intelligence.

It all works because each element knows the part it has to play, working towards a common goal, survival, and each is empowered to do it. It's a great system of accountability. It's another reason why organizations need to work effectively with risk.

Accountability and the 'agency' problem – whose risk is it?

Taleb suggests that the factor that most stands in the way of organizations being anti-fragile is the 'Agency' problem. This is about un-aligned accountability and is one of the issues we addressed in our research on risk (West et al., 2014). It's about the fact that organizational managers don't have enough 'skin in the game' for them to care enough about the risks that an organization faces. Personal risk is not aligned with organizational risk.

We see this quite starkly in the story of Nick Leeson, who brought about the demise of Barings Bank through his trading actions – as portrayed in the film *Rogue Trader*. He ran the bank's Singapore office and, at one point, tried to cover up an error by one of his young team by trading out of the loss. The first time he did it, the market moved against him, and he ended up with an even bigger loss on the books. He was able to hide this from Barings HQ, and bet on another bigger speculative trade, which if it had worked would be enough to wipe out the hidden loss accumulated so far. But that one also went the wrong way. As he traded bigger and bigger amounts to cover up previous losses, the market continued to go against him. Eventually he had a loss of over a billion dollars, which he could no longer hide and Barings bank was taken down as it had to be exposed. He had single-handedly bankrupted the bank.

It looks like Leeson was an idiot, but actually in a sense he behaved quite rationally. For him, while the upside potentially increased if he pulled off the trade as being a bit of a hero, locally at least, the downside remained more or less the same for subsequent trades – he would lose his job and reputation, and probably go to gaol. So there was a consistent rational motivation for him to continue to trade. However, for the bank as a whole, the upside didn't improve much relatively, but at each trade, the potential loss doubled and the possibility of bankruptcy loomed progressively closer.

While this is an extreme example, this mismatch of risk accountability plays out in the vast majority of private sector organizations. In banks generally, senior managers are rewarded for positive results, but generally don't face the consequences of adverse results. Even if they end up leaving a poorly performing bank, they generally leave with much greater financial rewards than the shareholders, who are ultimately you and I, the general public, through our pension plans and endowment policies. Similar stories are played out in other organizations.

As my colleague Eve Poole (2015) has pointed out, this is the basis of another toxic assumption in the capitalist system, that risk and reward is distributed fairly and sensibly across stakeholders of a business. There is a growing case for revisiting the mutual business model – where all business stakeholders share equitably in the risks and rewards experienced by the business. Then business strategies are more likely to be taking on the right risks.

But even before we get to radical changes in business models, there is a case for broadening accountability for risk. If you remember, one of the illusions we covered in Chapter 7 (Section 'Risk management') was that of risk management itself. This is the idea that you can somehow manage risk by delegating it away, to a respectable manager who has been given the title 'Head of Risk, or to the Risk Committee' or even the Finance Director. From there, it can all be managed with risk analysis, or risk assessments or risk modelling. While all of this may be helpful to some degree, particularly to elephants, the problem is that it promotes the myth that I, as a manager in the business, no longer need to be concerned about risk. It can work different ways: either I become more risk averse, because in doing that, I am protecting my own skin, or, like Nick Leeson, I become more risk taking, because I can gain from the upside without losing from the downside.

There is evidence of a move away from this distorted view. More businesses are talking about 'enterprise risk management', and while some interpret this as spreading risk analysis and process more widely across the organization in a bureaucratic way, others see it as spreading accountability for risk. And with that, improved capability to understand and work with risk. The role of the Enterprise Risk Management function then becomes more one of co-ordination and skills development, rather than one of imposing additional bureaucracy.

A recent *Harvard Business Review* article entitled 'How to live with risk' picked up on this theme (CEB, 2015). It explains: 'The goal is to transform risk management from a peripheral function to one with a voice integrated into day-to-day management. Leading companies view every decision they make as a risk decision [and] choose their risks with great calculation'. It talks of factoring a better understanding of risk into decision making. 'At Lego, for instance, the senior director of strategic risk management is included in all decisions involving capital above a certain amount. He helps colleagues to spot potential problems and managers see how their projects fit into the company's overall portfolio of projects, each with its own set of risks.' He concludes by noting that it is less about listing risks from a backward-looking perspective and more about picking the right portfolio of risky projects.

Another interesting aspect of what this article proposes is a change in the perception of what risk is – moving away from the idea that it is all about avoiding danger, and towards seeing risk as variability with an aspect of opportunity attached to it.

The same article quotes that: 'Fully 60% of the corporate strategy officers surveyed said that their company's decision-making process is too slow, in part because of an excessive focus on preventing risk. They added that if this "organizational drag" were reduced, the rate of revenue growth might double. Just 20 per cent described their companies as "risk seeking."'

Another message from the article is that 'risk management' is often synonymous with 'risk prevention'. But as any portfolio manager knows, lower risk often means lower returns. Today's risk managers see their role as helping firms determine and clarify their appetite for risk and communicate it across the company to guide decision making. In some cases this means helping line managers reduce their risk aversion. For example, one large company decided to terminate the policy of a client it had insured for thirty-five years. The client wasn't very risky, so profits on its policy were negligible.

One of our retailers in the modern slavery research project advised us that they don't have a risk function or even a separate Risk Committee involving board directors. This is because they take the view that leaders throughout the organization need to be accountable for risk. In the case of our respondent, in running a function focussed on supply chain ethics, he had a direct reporting line to non-executive directors, and regular enquiries from major shareholders, who were particularly interested in the ethical risks associated with the supply chain.

Accountability for both ethical and commercial risk was a particular challenge in the global retail supply chain, as we discovered in our research on modern slavery. This had major implications for the style of leadership, which in one respondent's eyes needed to be a balance of being prudent and being brave. Challenging manufacturers in China and Cambodia about their working practices was not for the faint-hearted, nor the reckless.

One of the other dynamics we are more likely to see in this kind of organization is an openness to risky conversations.

Risky conversations

It seems that somehow at the heart of how organizations work with risk is the types of conversations that happen between its members. My Organization Development consulting colleagues at Ashridge tell me that culture change happens one conversation at a time. I am very impressed by this concept, and have witnessed it playing out both with clients with whom we work and in the extensive change we have seen at Ashridge over the past four years.

I was working recently with a global services client. There were over a hundred of them, from the top team downwards, and they had all come from different parts of the world to a classy conference centre in west London. The day started with a strategy presentation, and then the result of a culture assessment exercise. We had proposed and agreed with the top team that they would have a better chance of succeeding with the strategy if they were able to change their culture. There were many aspects to it, but a couple of key ones were a move from one that prioritizes individual technical performance at the expense of relationship with colleagues, to one which places more emphasis on relationship and behavioural factors; to one that values being 'heard' above the one that currently puts a greater value on being 'right'. Then we asked them to sit in groups, made up of mixed levels of management. We observed and facilitated.

Initially, most of the voices in the groups were those of the most senior managers expressing their views on technical solutions associated with the strategy. By the end of the day, we were hearing some of the lower levels of management expressing views about human behavioural issues, sometimes even critical of current practices.

We asked them to reflect on what had happened in the room. Initially, they talked about the technical solutions they had come up with. Then, with a bit of coaxing, they started to notice how the conversations had changed in the groups. People were taking risks in conversations: senior managers inviting their more junior colleagues to be open with their views; more junior managers making non-technical points, even being critical of leadership behaviours.

Somehow the managers in this room had become more convinced that they all had similar 'skin in the game', and therefore it was worth taking personal risks to speak out. This was a step towards a more anti-fragile organization. Weick and Sutcliffe wrote a book *Highly Resilient Organisations* (HROs) (Weick & Sutcliffe, 2007), and unpick some of their characteristics – what works and what doesn't work in terms of making them more or less resilient. These are organizations that are regularly dealing with crisis or the potential for crisis (e.g. emergency service or the military). Many factors can impact resilience, but the one stand-out factor seems to be the ability to be open with failure, to talk about it, to consider its possibility, to be honest about its occurrence, and to consider how it could be avoided or managed if and when it happens.

When we did our research on risk, one of the senior managers of an organization responsible for regulating financial risk told me that, prior to the banking crisis, the ongoing assumption was that risk management and modelling could predict crisis and therefore, if the right measures were in place, stop it happening. He no longer believed in this. Instead, his view was that the only way to deal effectively with risk is to have people talk about it a lot.

But even talking about it can feel risky. One of the conundrums I have discovered is that those who work well with risk do so because actually they feel safe with it. How so?

Chapter 13

Feeling safe with risk

One of my stated aims from this book is to help leaders feel safe with risk. This is of course a paradox, yet I believe the reality is that leaders will not take the risks they need to take if they don't feel safe in doing so. This is looking under the bonnet of the leader, to understand what might be going on behind the scenes to support right risk taking. Up to now, we have been looking at the outward evidence of risk-taking decisions in organizations, with some exploration of what psychological factors might influence those decisions. But the deeper issue is how risk makes you feel when you take it, particularly personal risk.

Some would argue that it's the lack of safety in risk which creates the buzz for risk takers. There is some aspect of the impact of our hormones which can deliver a high when we flirt with danger. Chapter 6 (Section 'Physiological factors') on the physiology of risk talked about the winner effect created by an increase in the level of testosterone. But risks taken just for the buzz are in danger of being the wrong kinds of risk, for the kinds of leadership roles that we are talking about and particularly for strategic decision making.

Yet I believe at some level, right risk takers do have a mechanism for helping them to feel safe. Part of this may indeed be the hormonal effect which not only prepares us with the capabilities to engage more effectively with risk, as in the case of testosterone, but also provides an anaesthetic to numb the fear. The idea of feeling safe with risk is one of the bases on which we have tried to offer executive education at Ashridge.

In helping leaders to develop, the challenge is to help them understand both the formal and informal aspects of risk, and to use that understanding to make skilful choices in their working lives. But there is a conundrum. In traditional teaching environments, away from the buzz of everyday working life, how do we replicate the real risks that leaders face, in the relatively 'safe' environment of the classroom? Conceptualizing risk for learning purposes appears to have an anaesthetizing impact on our actual experience of it. We may think our way through a case study involving risk in an abstract way, using suitable models to help us, but the emotion of risk is generally missing in a safe environment. Virtually nothing we do or say in a classroom setting will put the company finances at risk, nor affect the health of our stakeholders or our own careers. To some extent, this is exactly why the classroom is designed to be a safe environment – it's confidential. What happens in the room, stays in the room.

Indeed, the unique selling proposition for 'away-from-the-workplace' learning is that it is a safe environment in which to experiment, in which to take some risks that participants wouldn't normally take in the workplace. These risks can be about exploring and articulating new ideas to colleagues, about having conversations that they wouldn't normally have, or about interacting with others in a way that may not feel comfortable. So for some aspects of working with risk, the classroom offers an advantage, even if it may feel a little artificial or clinical.

But, paradoxically, if we are creating safety to work with risk, how can this be authentic?

We have successfully worked around this dilemma in our management development practice by using simulations that generate the emotion of risk. These take the form either of team-based competitive decision making in a computerized marketplace simulation over a series of rounds, or of working through specific artificial challenges working with professional actors, whose role it is to re-create some of the emotion of difficult, risky situations. Participants have also been asked to wear heart rate monitors over one or two days, as they work together to resolve simulated problems which may be creating tensions between individuals. Participants are encouraged to experiment with roles that are different from those they would normally have, and with types of interventions that they would typically not employ. Their emotional responses are monitored and measured.

These programmes demonstrate that they can have a significant residual learning impact – that is, this learning manifests itself after, not during, the experience of the programme. Participants start to apply certain aspects of what they have experimented with on the programme back at work and they are encouraged, post-programme, to reflect and to continue learning from these reflections. They effectively build on the risk that they have already taken during the programme by applying the experiment in a real work environment. There is effectively a physiological stress memory, reflected in the heart rate printout, which gets replayed in the workplace. This has been called the development of emotional muscle memory, in the same way that a tennis player only really learns how to hit an effective tennis shot when he does it automatically without having to think about it – that is, when he has developed muscle memory.

We believe that the simulations of the emotions associated with risk help participants to develop skill in the management of informal risk, by experiencing the emotions and intuitions associated with them, reflecting and then transferring that muscle memory to the workplace.

So hormones are one factor that can help us to feel safe with risk. Experimentation and the development of risk-taking muscle memory is another. Faith is yet another. I believe that leaders take risk by putting faith in a range of different people and things. Sometime it's the power of a logical argument, or the evidence from a pattern of information. And sometimes it's belief in another individual or group of individuals.

The role of faith

So in handling this paradox of safety with risk, our approach to risk will of course be determined by where or how you experience safety. We tend to experience safety where we can truly place our faith.

I am reminded of the exploits of the Niagara Falls tight rope walker in the mid-nineteenth century known as 'The Great Blondin', whose real name was Jean Francois Gravelet. He repeated the stunt of crossing the falls on many occasions, sometimes using other props, like bicycles and wheelbarrows. On one occasion, he is reputed to have taunted the crowd with the question: 'How much do you believe in me?' and getting loud affirmation. He then asked who in the crowd who said they believed in him would get on his back as he crossed the falls. No one was prepared to do that – no one had that much faith in him. He did apparently eventually do it with his own manager, which caused quite a stir not just for the crowd but also for the manager.

How can you feel safe with risk? To whom or what can you put enough faith to feel safe?

- For some it's more in numbers and logic – the evidence is enough.
- For some it's in relationships – and knowing that certain key people are in the same place as me.
- For some it's in intuition and gut – I know it down deep – it's a whole body experience.
- For some it's in a belief or world view – perhaps a cultural or religious view which also informs values.

My initial interest in exploring the subject of risk in leadership was shepherded by another related interest – the role of faith in business. I have for some time been fascinated by how some people make quite difficult decisions, on issues involving quite high levels of uncertainty, with an almost equally high degree of confidence. I am particularly fascinated when this happens with leaders in business. And I would tend to express this confidence as faith. Normally there is some object of that faith, and actually the real sentiment attaching that leader to that object of faith is trust.

So what are those objects of faith, those factors on which a leader bases a decision and which is the source of confidence? They can be a number of things. First and foremost, they can and often are other people. I will take this decision because I trust you; either that you have done your homework adequately in recommending this decision in the first place; or that in going with this plan of action, I can trust you will make sure that it happens the way it needs to. So my faith in taking this decision is in another person or group of people.

I have some experience of working with private equity investors and venture capitalists. They take decisions involving risk all the time – that is their business calling. They will review business plans, take positions on certain technologies and market sectors, and meet the proposed teams that will be leading the ventures that are requesting funding. The single biggest factor that will determine whether or not to invest in that venture is what they think of the management team. Essentially it is: do they trust them to do what they say they are going to do in the business plan? The investors are primarily basing their risky decisions on whether or not to invest, on whether or not they have faith in the management team.

Leaders can also base their faith on other factors. A strong well-reasoned argument with good supporting evidence can also be a basis for faith. This can be especially true where this forms part of a proven process. This was the culture of decision making at Procter & Gamble (P&G), where I joined as a trainee marketing manager, straight out of business school. P&G has a culture of encouraging new young business managers (brand managers, market managers) to take ownership for a small portion of the business and take initiatives that require decisions involving some degree of business risk. The primary process for doing this was that juniors like me wrote proposals – often famously no more than one page long – which were submitted, approved and forwarded to increasingly higher levels of management, until they were finally approved for implementation at the appropriately highest level, quite often either the regional general manager, or the president of the division, which in my case was P&G's export and special operations division, headquartered in Geneva, Switzerland.

I remember meeting my regional general manager for the first time after I joined. He gave me a few tips. One of them was that when I submit a proposal for some kind of investment, if the decision comes down to a difference between his opinion and mine, his would always win. But if it came down to his opinion, and a well-reasoned and evidenced argument on my part, mine would win. Leaders at P&G place a high level of faith in evidence and logic, not to the exclusion of faith in individuals, but the evidence is a major contributor. And of course, because this is part of the P&G culture, the two go very much hand in hand.

We know people place their faith in a name. Customers make daily decisions on product or service purchases based on brand names. There is risk in any purchase – we often cannot be sure that the product or service that we pay money for will deliver what it is supposed to. This is the basis of branding. P&G launched the first branded soap, Ivory, in the mid-nineteenth century because they noticed that unscrupulous soap makers were supplying poor quality soap to customers – the kind that would just disintegrate after a couple of washes, for example. So you bought your soap from a vendor you trusted – you placed your faith in the person. But as markets got bigger and more impersonal, you couldn't do this any more. Every purchase was a risk that you were buying a soap that would disintegrate. So P&G created a soap with a quality-controlled process, and marked it with a name, a brand name, Ivory. As it happens the brand name was inspired by Psalm 45: 'From palaces adorned with *ivory*, the music of the strings makes you glad'. Here was a soap you could trust – a brand name you could put your faith in, one that effectively mitigated the risk of the purchase.

On a larger scale, where risk is a more blatant issue, faith in a brand still plays a significant role. Consider IBM and the mantra that echoed around the corridors of power in many organizations: 'At least you won't get sacked for buying IBM'. Similar stories could be told of other major service business-to-business brands. 'We are confident in this difficult decision because McKinsey or PwC have recommended it.'

My interest in this approach was also kindled by a conversation with a colleague, on leadership in sustainability, and a particular example from Coca-Cola. They became aware that one opportunity to generate significant energy savings and environmental benefits was to put doors on their coolers in retail outlets. And yet they also knew from research that doing this would have a significant adverse impact on sales and profit. So what was the underlying leadership mindset that led them to put doors on all their retail coolers? I was interested in how leaders saw faith as playing a role in leadership and I saw the link between risk and faith.

Cultural and religious influences

When we explore the origins of the word 'risk', we find it is inextricably linked to cultural and religious belief systems.

Clyne, whose paper 'Etymology of Risk' (2004) sparked off some of our thinking around the different definitions of risk, picked up this aspect from the heritage of the word. Historically, it is shrouded in mythology, associated with philosophy and religion – 'the domain of the gods'. At one point, the character of the risk taker was considered more important than the outcome. Taking risk was often considered a virtue and associated with courage. Only in more recent times has the avoidance of risk, encapsulated in the word 'prudence' been also seen as a virtue. The concept seems to be two sided, with one side statistical and the other based on personal principles and belief.

Breakwell in the *Psychology of Risk* (2014) has similar reflections, but a slightly different spin. She says that the common usage of the word 'risk' in Europe coincides with an erosion of belief in divine determination of the individual's fate and a decline in the power of organized religion in the face of sectarianism and the growth of nation states. She believes it came to be used in commercial contexts. For instance, it was used by merchants who needed to represent the likelihood of a cargo arriving in port safely. It evolved into a central concept in scientific and engineering discourse – the assessment of the probability of failure in a physical system, and then, subsequently, of the probability that a physical system might generate harm are essential ingredients of applied science.

Risk has been central to some of the more interesting debates in the social sciences over recent years. In effect, risk has been released from the sole ownership of the physical sciences, where it was treated as something that should be assessed and estimated quantitatively – if only the right tools could be developed. Instead, it has been captured by philosophers, political scientists, sociologists, geographers, social anthropologists and psychologists, who have all brought their own critical lenses to the conceptualization of risk.

Chapter 14
Conclusion: The Jenga tower

The cover of this book depicts a Jenga tower, a game which is popular with adults and children alike, in which players take it in turn to add a brick to the top to make the tower taller. The catch is that the brick added at the top has to come from within the tower. And the primary aim is to do this without the tower collapsing.

Jenga is a metaphor for what I have been describing as the essence of risky strategy. First of all, it highlights the issues of winning. Normally the winner is the one who doesn't make the tower fall down. This works if there are only two players. If you have more than two, you can only identify a loser, the person who causes the tower to collapse.

While there is an element of fun in this, if I'm honest, I don't particularly enjoy this version of the game. You see, the best I can achieve is to not be the loser, but every time I take my turn, I risk causing the tower to collapse. It speaks to my loss aversion. This says that, even in a two-player game, I am much more concerned about the possibility of losing than I am excited about the prospect of being the winner. But in a three-player game, I don't even have the possibility of being the winner – there is only a loser.

But then there is another possibility that often emerges in this game. The players decide, either explicitly or implicitly, that the real aim is to build the record highest tower. If they can achieve this, then everyone is a winner. It becomes collaboration rather than competition. Another way to look at this is that the people around the tower are no longer competitors; the competitor is another team somewhere else also trying to build a Jenga tower. Our real risk then is the variability in the laws of physics – the right amount of friction on the bricks. Too much, and you can't push the bricks out of the lower part of the tower; too little and the bricks are less able to keep the tower from collapsing.

So how else is Jenga a useful metaphor for risky strategy?

We have limited resources, so we have to make tough choices – that is the source of the risk. We have to remove a brick from the existing structure, and this process is what can cause the ultimate failure, the collapse of the tower.

But we can mitigate that risk. First, we can mitigate by Informing: we can test a brick by nudging first and gauging what happens. If it seems to slide without friction we push more. We can mitigate by sharing. Others can help in removing the brick.

Sometimes we progress by nudging, testing and collaborating – an analytical social elephant approach. Sometime we look at the tower and we have a sense of the best place to pick the next brick from, and our confidence in our ability to grow the tower grows with every brick. We move into the intuitive tiger zone.

But at the end of the day, however careful or insightful we are, the height of the tower ultimately will most likely depend on one fundamental factor: the foundation on which the tower is built. If we build on a solid flat base, we can expect to achieve a good height. If we build on a soft base like a carpet or an uneven floor, we will struggle to achieve the same height. Our foundation is our organizational character, and our risk taking is based on our faith to build on a solid base.

For such a time as this

Today, we are witnessing Jenga towers toppling and collapsing, towers that previously looked strong. Others on firmer foundations remain strong. And new towers are being built all the time.

In our research on modern slavery, we have reached a situation where businesses at the end of complex global supply chains, primarily the big brand retailers, are in a position to impact positively on the welfare of millions of workers in and from developing countries. Historically, these businesses have competed to offer the best deal for consumers in the developed nations. This is the essence of the capitalist model as originally set out by Adam Smith in his eighteenth-century book *The Wealth of Nations* (1997). We have international legislation that fiercely protects this competitive principle, on the basis that it protects the 'paying public' from exploitation.

However, we know today that in return for this privilege, there is still exploitation of workers that contributes to delivering this consumer benefit. We know from our research that the only reasonable ways in which the developed world's retailers and other major corporates can change this for the better is by collaborating – to maximize the influence and impact where it matters, including with national governments. Ironically, in the UK and other countries, the latest legislation on modern slavery is a catalyst that encourages this collaboration. But this flies in the face of naturally competitive instincts and competition law. Is this a time for bold leaders to challenge this paradigm? Could this be a time for a positive Black Swan?

Indeed, is this a time for business to become part of the solution, instead of part of the problem?

Timothy Fort, Professor of Ethics at George Washington University Business School, and Director of that university's programme on 'Peace through Commerce' (2007), argues that for such a time as this, business itself has a role to play in bringing ethical leadership to the world in which it has become a core element. He develops classical 'theory of the firm' thinking: is the purpose of business to maximize shareholder value, which gets further translated and simplified to maximize profit, or is it fundamentally to bring about positive social change?

In Chapter 7, when I described the concept of broad framing, I listed Paul Polman's vision for Unilever as bringing positive social benefit to the world's consumers – the broad framing was that this would ultimately generate positive value to shareholders, even if the short-term picture was less clear. My old company, and Unilever arch-rival, Procter & Gamble, also articulated one of their 'Winning Aspirations' along similar lines: 'To meaningfully improve the lives of the world's consumers' (Lafley & Martin, 2013).

A recent interview reported by McKinsey, highlighted in the following box, indicates that Novartis are also developing a different perspective on what they aspire to do, one which involves having the courage to do 'what's right' – taking the right risk!

> *Novartis is also elevating some values that reflect the way society is chang-*
> *ing... Having the courage to try and to fail... And the final one is integrity,*
> *because society's expectations about healthcare companies have shifted over*
> *time. Doing what's legal is not enough. We have to do what's right.*
>
> *Joseph Jimenez, CEO of Novartis*

It is aspects of character, and the principles that drive leadership decisions, that ultimately determine the risky strategies that need to be
taken. In the Ashridge research on 'How leaders work with risk', the
chief executive of a major hospital trust told me that he was making
decisions involving some element of risk on a daily basis. Asked how he
evaluated those decisions, the single most important factor was his
own personal values. In a recent case, he found himself making a decision contrary to the opinion of board colleagues, which was highly
unpopular more widely. But he knew, based on the evidence he had,
that it was the right thing to do. He was able to make the decision with
a clear conscience, but at the same time attracted significant adverse
publicity, which, for ethical reasons, he was not able to address overtly.
This had personal risk consequences, but these were outweighed by the
bigger corporate risks that he saw.

The management of risk lies at the heart of banking practice and the
financial services industry operates a scientific model to address this. In
2008, the Financial Services Authority (FSA) in the UK had developed a
highly sophisticated computer-based model for assessing and measuring risk. It is now generally accepted that this model failed to anticipate
the banking crisis – that is, it failed to manage the risk effectively. But
some commentators argue that the real failure was the questionable
nature of the underpinning values prevalent in the industry, combined
with a lack of challenge to the widespread risk-taking practices, which
were regarded as acceptable by many working in the sector.

T. R. Malloch (2013) in his book *The End of Ethics... and a Way Back* lists a
number of ethical failures in the financial services industry, both before
and after the crisis. He quotes Kevin Rudd, the Australian Prime
Minister who said, in a speech he called 'The children of Gordon Gekko':

Beneath the financial jargon and dramatic stock market events, the sub-prime crisis has also reflected a fundamental failure of values. We have seen the triumph of greed over integrity; the triumph of speculation over value creation; the triumph of the short term over the long-term sustainable growth.

The 'ethical shortcomings' that appear to have contributed, at least in part, to the banking crisis don't seem to have stopped. They have continued to happen in guises such as LIBOR rate-fixing, money laundering and tax avoidance, to name but a few. The ongoing failings in financial services and other sectors seem to confirm there is a bigger issue than just having a big sophisticated computer system for managing risk.

The disastrous consequences of the global recession for countries and businesses demand that we find a new paradigm for dealing with ethical issues. To protect national economies and to ensure that businesses thrive within them, we must acknowledge that ethics are increasingly on the agenda for business, and therefore for business leaders, and therefore for business schools. Research conducted by Carrington Crisp, a research company specializing in business education (2013), found that clients of business schools saw the most important role of business schools was to 'develop business leaders with strong ethical behaviours'.

Thus, the attitude and approach that leaders take to risk can relate to their personal values and approach to ethics. It's a key issue which was identified in 'The Tone from the Top' reporting research that was conducted in 2013 with the chairmen of 30 UK organizations. The research looked at how boards provide ethical leadership to their organizations. This report developed the idea that boards can set an ethical tone by their own behaviour and by how they signal ethical priorities – for example, in what kind of person is either recruited or promoted, or by how information is shared. The report links this back to organizational risk, arguing that a board's approach to ethical issues has a direct bearing on 'ethical risk', which is effectively the 'reputational risk' of non-ethical behaviour amongst managers.

One of our prospective clients is currently embarking on a global culture change programme entitled 'courageous integrity'. The issue that was described was born out of the observation that people put on different persona when they come to work from the persona that they wear at home. They wanted a programme to encourage a culture that embraced sustainable integrity, but recognized that it required bravery on the part of individuals to pull this off.

One of the concluding points from Collins and Hansen's (2011) work on leaders of successful organizations was:

> When the moment comes when we're afraid, exhausted or tempted – what choice do we make? Do we abandon our values? ... Do we give up on our dreams when we've been slammed by brutal facts? The greatest leaders we've studied throughout all our research cared as much about values as victory, as much about purpose as profit, as much about being useful as being successful. We are not imprisoned by our circumstances. We are not imprisoned by the luck we get or the inherent unfairness of life ... In the end, we can control only a tiny sliver of what happens to us. But even so, we are free to choose, free to become great by choice.

I like some of the thinking from Osho's *Courage – The Joy of Living Dangerously* (Osho, 1999, St. Martin's Griffin, ISBN 0-312-20517-1). He says about uncertainty: 'Don't call it uncertainty – call it wonder'. He is alert to dogma, and says: 'The way of the heart is the way of courage. It is to live in insecurity; it is to live in love, and trust ... a person who is alive, really alive, vitally alive, will always move into the unknown. There is danger there, but he will take the risk.'

However, he implies that the heart is to be prioritized over the head, almost that the head is of limited value. I disagree. It seems to me that we have both so we should use both. This excites the tiger in me, but I don't want to slay the elephant in the process.

We need tigers: they are colourful, fast off the mark and make our lives interesting in an exciting unpredictable kind of way. They are indeed the heartbeat behind innovation. They are bold and creative pioneers. But they can be chaotic, too. They can be loners, more than leaders. And left alone to work, they can become reckless, taking the wrong risk.

So we also need elephants, as although they may be slow and perhaps a little dull, they are methodical and sure-footed. They are social, so they work well with others, and create momentum. They can dull the sharp edges of risk by becoming better informed and building consensus, and by finding the ways to share risk around. They can be specialists in Empathy and specialists in Self-Discipline. Or both. But left for too long in their comfortable modes, they can become champions of risk avoidance. They can shrink in stature and become quite cowardly.

So at the end of the day, we need tigers!

Leaders need to be able to encourage both tigers and elephants. Better still, they need to tap into the tiger and the elephant in themselves. They need to be able to exploit character, whether that's Bold Creativity, Empathy or Self-Discipline. They need to understand where and in whom they put their faith, which allows them to feel safe in taking the right risks. It's my contention that these leaders will develop the best strategies, strategies that are more likely to define and achieve winning aspirations – whether winning means beating the market competition or, better still, beating the hidden enemies that stand in the way of making our world a better place in which to live.

Juxtaposed in the tensions – working with the dilemmas

This book has been a journey of discovery, and probably the most significant discovery has been how my concept of Creative Juxtaposition is at the heart of risky strategy. It's an idea that is very much the cousin of Duggan's 'Strategic Intuition', who in turn has built on von Clausewitz 'coup d'oeil'. It's the idea that good strategy is generally bold and creative, while avoiding being reckless and destructive. That it often comes as a result of combining selective knowledge from different sources with intuition, a moment of inspiration even, which builds confidence, and makes the risk seem safe.

It's a story within a story. Our main characters, the elephant and the tiger, the formal analytical and the informal intuitive, respectively, are very different in character, but when they combine, a creative explosion can happen.

And these come within a bigger Creative Juxtaposition story – my own bold venture in writing this, my first book. In putting my hand up at Ashridge to contribute to this new business book series with Bloomsbury, I didn't have a complete piece of research on which to base the book. I had pieces of research, my own experience, books I had read on the subject and a rough idea of what I wanted to say.

I set out on a journey to combine two fairly meaty well-documented subjects, that of strategy, which has been the basis of my expertise as a consultant over much of my career, and that of risk, which has been the subject of our research here at Ashridge. The journey has been to combine these two giant subjects in Creative Juxtaposition to see what would emerge – to trust to the intuition, to expect the inspiration, and to be bold enough to commit them to writing and publishing.

Bibliography

Ansoff, I. (1965). *Corporate Strategy*. London: Penguin.

Bono, E. d. (1999). *Six Thinking Hats*. London: Penguin.

Breakwell, G. M. (2014). *The Psychology of Risk*. Cambridge: Cambridge University Press.

Bungay, S. (2011). *The Art of Action*. London: Nicolas Brealey Publishing.

Buytendijk, F. (2010). *Dealing with Dilemmas: Where Business Analytics Fall Short*. New Jersey: John Wiley & Sons.

Campbell, A., Finklestein, S., & Whitehead, J. (2008). *Think Again*. Boston: Harvard Business Press.

Carrington Crisp. (2013). *See the Future 2013*. London: Carrington Crisp.

CEB. (2015, July–August). How to live with risk. *Harvard Business Review, 93*, 20–21.

Christensen, C. M. (2002). *The Innovator's Dilemma: The Revolutionary Book That Will Change the Way You Do Business*. New York: HarperCollins.

Clarke, D. I. (1993). *The Man with the Key Has Gone!* Chichester: New Wine Press.

Clausewitz, C. v. (1976). *On War*. Edited and Translated by Michael Howard and Peter Paret. Princeton: Princeton University Press.

Cline, P. (2004). *The Etymology of Risk*. Portsmouth: Harvard.

Coates, J. (2012). *The Hour Between Dog and Wolf: How Risk Taking Transforms Us, Body and Mind*. London: Penguin-Random House.

Collins, J. (2001). *Good to Great: Why Some Companies Make the Leap ... and Others Don't*. London: Random House.

Collins, J., & Hansen, M. (2011). *Great by Choice*. New York: Random House Group.

Confino, J. (2012, April 24). Unilever's Paul Polman: Challenging the status quo. *Guardian Sustainable Business*. Retrieved from http://www.theguardian.com/sustainable-business/paul-polman-unilever-sustainable-living-plan

Courtney, H. (2001). *2020 Foresight – 'Crafting strategy in an Uncertain World'*. Boston: Harvard Business School Publishing.

Dickens, C. (1859). *A Tale of Two Cities*.

Duggan, W. (2007). *Strategic Intuition*. New York: Columbia University Press.

Eldredge, J. (2001). *Wild at Heart: Discovering the Secret of a Man's Soul*. Nashville: Thomas Nelson.

Ferguson, A. (2013). *My Autobiography*. London: Hodder & Stoughton.

Firestein, S. (2012). *Ignorance: How It Drives Science*. New York: Oxford University Press.

Fort, T. L. (2007). *Business, Integrity and Peace (Business, Value Creation, and Society)*. Cambridge: Cambridge University Press.

Gerstner, L. V. (2002). *Who Says Elephants Can't Dance?: Leading a Great Enterprise Through Dramatic Change*. New York: HarperCollins.

Gifford, J. (2010). *History Lessons: What Business and Management Can Learn from the Great Leaders of History*. London: Marshall Cavendish.

Gladwell, M. (2006). *Blink: The Power of Thinking Without Thinking*. London: The Penguin Group.

Goodwin, P., & Wright, G. (2004). *Decision Analysis for Management Judgement*. Chichester: John Wiley & Sons.

Gray, C. S. (2009). *Fighting Talk: Forty Maxims on War, Peace and Strategy*. Dulles: Potomac Books.

Hamel, G., & Prahalad, C. (1990). The core competence of the corporation. *Harvard Business Review, 68*(3), 79–91.

Hammer, M., & Champy, J. (1991). *Reengineering the Corporation: A Manifesto for Business Revolution*. New York: HarperCollins.

Johnson, G., Whittington, R., Scholes, K., Angwin, D., & Regner, P. (2014). *Exploring Strategy: Text and Cases*. Harlow: Pearson Education Limited.

Kahler, T. (1975). Drivers – The key to the process script. *Transactional Analysis Journal, 5*, 3.

Kahneman, D. (2011). *Thinking, Fast and Slow*. London: Allen Lane, Penguin Books.

Kim, W., & Mauborgne, R. (2005). *Blue Ocean Strategy*. Boston: Harvard Business Review Press.

Knight, F. H. (1921). *Risk, Uncertainty and Profit*. Boston: Houghton Mifflin.

Kuhn, T. (1962). *The Structure of Scientific Revolutions*. Chicago: University of Chicago Press.

Lafley, A., & Martin, R. L. (2013). *Playing to Win: How Strategy Really Works*. Boston: Harvard Business Review Press.

Lake, Q., MacAlister, J., Berman, C., Gitsham, M., & Page, N. (2015). *Corporate Approaches to Addressing Modern Slavery in Supply Chains: A Snapshot of Current Practice*. Hult International Business School; The Ethical Trading Initiative, The Ashridge Centre for Business and Sustainability. Ashridge Executive Education, Hult International Business School. Retrieved from https://ashridge.org.uk/faculty-research/research/current-research/research-projects/corporate-approaches-to-addressing-modern-slavery/

Leonard, R. (2010). *Von Neumann, Morgenstern and the Creation of Game Theory*. New York: Cambridge University Press.

MacAlister, J. (2015, Winter). Resolving Risky Leadership Dilemmas: How Character Profiling Can Help. *Developing Leaders*. Retrieved from http://www.iedp.com/magazine/2015issue18/index.html#32

Malloch, T. R. (2013). *The End of Ethics ... and a Way Back*. Singapore: John Wiley & Sons.

Mintzberg, H. (1994). *The Rise and Fall of Strategic Planning*. New York: Simon & Schuster.

Peplow, M. (2014). *Innovation: Managing Risk, Not Avoiding It: Evidence and Case Studies*. London: Government Office for Science.

Peters, T. J., & Waterman, Jr, R. H. (1982). *In Search of Excellence: Lessons from America's Best-Run Companies*. New York: Harper & Row.

Poole, E. (2015). *Capitalism's Toxic Assumptions: Redefining Next Generation Economics*. London: Bloomsbury Publishing.

Porter, M. E. (1980). *Competitive Strategy*. New York: Simon and Shuster.

Regester, M., & Larkin, J. (2005). *Risk Issues and Crisis Management*. London & Sterling VA: Kogan Page.

Ross, J. (2004). Pascal's legacy. *European Molecular Biology Organisation (EMBO) reports*.

Schisgall, O. (1981). *Eyes on Tomorrow: The Evolution of Procter & Gamble*. New York: J. G. Ferguson Publishing.

Schrage, M. (2000). *Serious Play: How the World's Best Companies Simulate to Innovate*. Boston: Harvard Business School Press.

Shakespeare, W. (c 1599). *The Complete Works of William Shakespeare: King Henry V*. New York: Nelson Doubleday.

Shaw, P., & Stacey, R. (2006). *Experiencing Risk, Spontaneity and Improvisation in Organizational Change*. Abingdon: Routledge.

Smith, A. (1997). *The Wealth of Nations*. London: Penguin.

Stoner, J. (1967). *Risky and Cautious Shifts in Group Decisions: The Influence of Widely Held Values*. Boston: Massachusetts Institute of Technology.

Syed, M. (2015). *Black Box Thinking: The Surprising Truth about Success*. London: John Murray.

Taleb, N. N. (2007). *Fooled by Randomness: The Hidden Role of Chance in Life and in the Markets*. London: Penguin.

Taleb, N. N. (2010). *The Black Swan – The Impact of the Highly Improbable*. New York: Random House.

Taleb, N. N. (2012). *Antifragile – How to Live in a World We Don't Understand*. London: Allen Lane - Penguin Books.

Teece, D. (2011). *Dynamic Capabilities and Strategic Management: Organising for Innovation and Growth*. Oxford: Oxford University Press.

Treacy, M., & Wiersema, F. (1995). *The Discipline of Market Leaders*. London: HarperCollins.

Treasurer, B. (2003). *Right Risk – 10 Powerful Principles for Taking Giant Leaps with Your Life*. San Francisco: Berrett-Koehler.

Unknown. (n.d.). *Burning Boats*. Retrieved from burningboats.com: http://burningboats.com/about-burningboatscom/

Van der Heijden, K. (1996). *Scenarios: The Art of Strategic Conversation*. Chichester: Wiley.

Weick, K., & Sutcliffe, K. M. (2007). *Managing the Unexpected: Resilient Performance in an Age of Uncertainty*. San Francisco: John Wiley & Sons.

Wernefelt, B. (1984). A resource-based view of the firm. *Strategic Management Journal, 5*(2), 171–180.

West, T., MacAlister, J., Mookherjee, D., & Brown, M. (2014). *Working with Risk: In Practice and in Principle: Lessons from the Field*. London: Ashridge Business School.

Index